Popular Complete Smart Series

• Advanced •
Complete
MathSmart®
Grade 3

Credits

Photos (Back Cover "girl on left"/123RF.com, "boy" Jose Manuel Gelpi Diaz/123RF.com, "girl in middle"/123RF.com, "girl on right" Paul Hakimata/123RF.com, "memo board" Sandra Van Der Steen/123RF.com)

Proud Sponsor of the Math Team of Canada 2017

 ISBN: 978-1-77149-201-0

ISBN: 978-1-77149-201-0

A Message to Parents

Advanced Complete MathSmart is an extension of our bestselling *Complete MathSmart* series. This series focuses on challenging word problems that require the application of the math concepts and skills that children have learned in the *Complete MathSmart* series.

The two sections in this book are designed to gradually develop your child's problem-solving and critical-thinking skills. In Section 1, each unit covers one core topic and begins with basic skills questions, followed by problem-solving questions that increase in difficulty as the unit progresses. It reinforces your child's math concepts and skills in the topic in focus. Working through this section, your child should be able to proficiently explain and illustrate the solutions to the word problems.

Section 2 provides abundant critical-thinking questions, each combining multiple topics from Section 1. The topics are integrated in different ways to provide a wide range of complex and challenging questions that help stimulate your child's mathematical reasoning and develop his or her critical-thinking skills.

An answer key with step-by-step solutions is also provided at the end of this comprehensive book. All the solutions are presented in a clear and organized way to allow your child to have a thorough understanding of the math concepts.

Advanced Complete MathSmart will not only improve your child's core math understanding and skills, but also develop his or her critical-thinking skills which are essential in solving daily life challenges.

Your Partner in Education,
Popular Book Co. (Canada) Ltd.

ISBN: 978-1-77149-201-0

Advanced Complete MathSmart®

Section 1:
Basic Problem-solving Questions

ISBN: 978-1-77149-201-0

Contents

Section 2:
Critical-thinking Questions

Level 1 – with hints

Level 2 – without hints

ISBN: 978-1-77149-201-0

ISBN: 978-1-77149-201-0

Section 1:
Basic Problem-solving Questions

ISBN: 978-1-77149-201-0

Addition

 **Math Skills**

①
$$95 + 56$$

②
$$413 + 99$$

③
$$524 + 393$$

④
$$695 + 878$$

⑤
$$819 + 374$$

⑥
$$928 + 575$$

⑦
$$495 + 980$$

⑧
$$675 + 525$$

⑨ 86 + 79 = _____

⑩ 213 + 95 = _____

⑪ 99 + 457 = _____

⑫ 127 + 729 = _____

⑬ 217 + 857 = _____

⑭ 146 + 847 = _____

⑮ 446 + 191 = _____

⑯ 772 + 790 = _____

⑰ 887 + 808 = _____

⑱ 184 + 957 = _____

⑲ Find the totals.

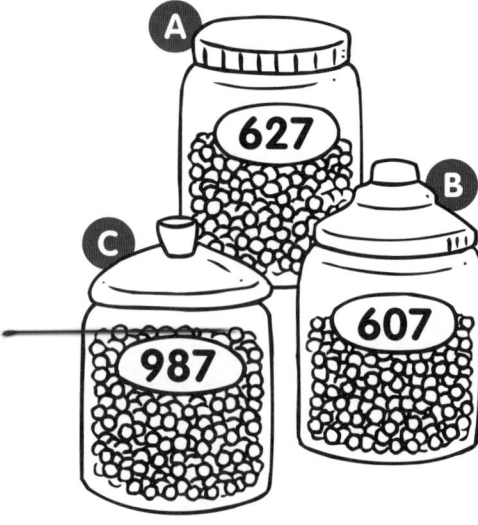

a. Jar A and Jar B:

_____ + _____ = _____ (candies)

b. Jar B and Jar C:

_____ + _____ = _____

c. Jar A and Jar C:

_____ + _____ = _____

ISBN: 978-1-77149-201-0

Problem Solving

Ralph collected 104 comic books. He got another 17 comic books. How many comic books does he have now?

Solution:

Step 1: Write a number sentence.

104 + 17 = ⬚

> Make sure the numbers align to the right.

Step 2: Do the addition.

```
  1 0 4
+    1 7
```
⬚

↑ Remember to add the carried "1".

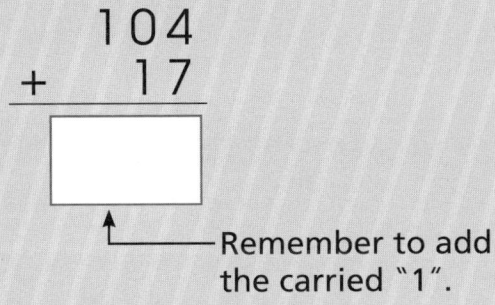

Step 3: Write a concluding sentence.

Ralph has ⬚ comic books now.

① There are 32 pages in a book. If Ralph reads 14 pages today and 17 pages tomorrow, will he finish reading his book tomorrow?

_____ , he _____ finish his book.
  Yes/No   will/will not

ISBN: 978-1-77149-201-0

② Nancy's Bakery bakes and sells cupcakes.

    a. A tray holds 24 cupcakes. The oven fits 2 trays. How many cupcakes can be baked at a time?

    _____ cupcakes can be baked at a time.

    b. 29 cupcakes were sold in the morning and 43 cupcakes were sold in the afternoon. How many cupcakes were sold in all?

    _____ cupcakes were sold in all.

    c.

> I earned $129 yesterday. Today, I earned $58 more than yesterday.

Nancy

How much money did Nancy earn in all?

Nancy earned $_____ in all.

💡 **Hints**

Read the questions carefully. Do not just add the two numbers.

ISBN: 978-1-77149-201-0

③ We are inviting 17 of my friends and 18 of Lori's friends to our birthday party.

Lori

Laura

a. Each friend needs 1 dinner plate. About how many plates are needed for the party?

About _____ plates are needed for the party.

b. How many plates are actually needed?

_____ plates are actually needed.

c. Each friend needs a fork and a spoon. How many forks and spoons are needed in total?

_____ forks and spoons are needed in total.

ISBN: 978-1-77149-201-0

④ Simon wants a new TV that costs $545. He has $235 and another $285 from selling his old TV. Does he have enough money?

_____

⑤ The students at Meadow Ridge Public School have different ways to get to school.

a. 2 buses arrive each morning. Each bus has 54 students. How many students take the bus?

_____

b. The remaining 276 students either walk or get a ride to school. How many students attend Meadow Ridge Public School?

_____

c.

> Westview Public School has 219 more students than Meadow Ridge Public School.

How many students attend Westview Public School?

_____

ISBN: 978-1-77149-201-0

⑥ Mr. Wilson is building a shed in his backyard.

a.

I have 219 wooden boards but I need 182 more.

Mr. Wilson

How many boards does he need in all?

402

b. Mr. Wilson also needs 1892 nails for the shed walls and 591 nails for the roof. Is one box of 2400 nails enough?

⑦ Susan's Shoes has stores in Springfield and Greenville.

a. The store in Springfield sold 719 pairs of sneakers and 517 pairs of sandals. How many pairs of shoes were sold?

b. The store in Greenville sold 175 pairs of sandals and 386 more sneakers than the store in Springfield. Which store sold more shoes?

$100 - 25 =$

⑧ Two airplanes landed at an airport. Each plane had 316 passengers. How many passengers arrived at the airport?

2

$$+ \begin{array}{r} 316 \\ 316 \\ \hline 632 \end{array} \qquad + \begin{array}{r} 200 \\ 112 \\ \hline 612 \end{array} \qquad - \begin{array}{r} 200 \\ 112 \\ \hline 312 \end{array} \qquad + \begin{array}{r} 531 \\ 248 \\ \hline 779 \end{array}$$

⑨ Fluffy the Cat finishes a bag of 288 cat treats in 1 week. How many cat treats will Fluffy eat in 3 weeks?

779

⑩ The scouts sold cookies to raise money for the hospital. Their goal was to raise $3250.

   a. Team A raised $929 and Team B raised $587. How much money did the two teams raise altogether?

   b. Team C raised $813 and Team D raised $335 more than Team B. Did Team C and Team D raise more money than Team A and Team B?

   c. Were the scouts able to raise enough money to reach their goal?

$1000 - 22 = 978$

ISBN: 978-1-77149-201-0

⑪

> I bike 1375 m on Main Street and 1084 m on Birch Street to get to a park.

Mike

a. How far does Mike need to bike to get to the park?

_____

b. Mike finds a new route that is 975 m on Oak Street and 1150 m on Maple Street. Is this route shorter than Mike's current route?

_____

⑫ The table shows the number of people who watched the two new movies.

a. How many people watched "Steelman" in the first two weeks?

Number of People That Watched Movies

Movie	Week 1	Week 2
Steelman	5038	4766
Outside In	5266	3441

_____

b. How many people watched one of the movies during Week 1?

_____

c. Which movie was more popular? Explain.

_____

ISBN: 978-1-77149-201-0

Subtraction

solving a variety of word problems that involve subtraction of 2- to 4-digit numbers

 **Math Skills**

①
$$\begin{array}{r} 90 \\ - 34 \\ \hline \end{array}$$

②
$$\begin{array}{r} 87 \\ - 19 \\ \hline \end{array}$$

③
$$\begin{array}{r} 96 \\ - 48 \\ \hline \end{array}$$

④
$$\begin{array}{r} 337 \\ - 53 \\ \hline \end{array}$$

⑤
$$\begin{array}{r} 672 \\ - 93 \\ \hline \end{array}$$

⑥
$$\begin{array}{r} 940 \\ - 71 \\ \hline \end{array}$$

⑦
$$\begin{array}{r} 616 \\ - 549 \\ \hline \end{array}$$

⑧
$$\begin{array}{r} 743 \\ - 526 \\ \hline \end{array}$$

⑨ 31 – 25 = _____

⑩ 78 – 49 = _____

⑪ 583 – 95 = _____

⑫ 816 – 417 = _____

⑬ 787 – 639 = _____

⑭ 606 – 284 = _____

⑮ 313 – 171 = _____

⑯ 555 – 467 = _____

⑰ 971 – 217 = _____

⑱ 833 – 454 = _____

⑲

Find the score differences.

My Scores

Round	Points
1	462
2	816
3	543

a. Round 1 and Round 2:

_____ – _____ = _____ (points)

b. Round 2 and Round 3:

_____ – _____ = _____ (points)

ISBN: 978-1-77149-201-0

Problem Solving

There are 80 children at a camp. 47 of them are canoeing. How many children are not canoeing?

Solution:

Step 1: **Write a number sentence.**

80 – 47 = _33_

Step 2: **Do the subtraction.**

```
   8 0
 – 4 7
   3 3
```

Don't forget to subtract 1 from the number you are borrowing from.

Step 3: **Write a concluding sentence.**

[   ] children are not canoeing.

① Refer to the question above. Of the children canoeing, 28 are boys. How many girls are canoeing?

_____ girls are canoeing.

ISBN: 978-1-77149-201-0

② Catherine had 60 stickers on her sticker sheet.

a. She used 32 stickers. How many stickers remain?

_____ stickers remain.

b. If Catherine gives 19 of the remaining stickers to her brother, how many stickers will be left?

_____ stickers will be left.

③ The Knights scored 94 points and the Bolts scored 79 points.

By how many points did the Knights win?

The Knights won by _____ points.

ISBN: 978-1-77149-201-0

④ Bus A has 75 passengers. Bus B has 55 passengers. How many more passengers are there on Bus A than on Bus B?

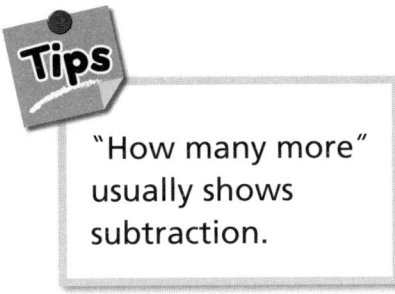

"How many more" usually shows subtraction.

There are _____ more passengers on Bus A.

⑤

I have $51. I want a pair of shoes that costs $39 but I need $10 to go home.

a. Estimate. If Arnold buys the shoes, will he have enough money to go home?

Arnold _____ have enough money to go home.
will/will not

b. How much money will Arnold actually have left after buying the shoes?

Arnold will have $_____ left.

ISBN: 978-1-77149-201-0

⑥

I scored 100 on my Math test!

Sam scored 27 more points than his last test. What was his last test score?

Sam

_____

⑦ Lucy wants to collect 200 pop tabs. She has collected 86 pop tabs so far. How many more pop tabs does she need to collect?

_____

⑧ 216 students attended the school concert. 87 of them were performers. How many students were in the audience?

_____

⑨ Louis has read 74 pages of his 331-page novel. How many more pages does he need to read to finish the book?

_____

ISBN: 978-1-77149-201-0

⑩ There are 311 people in a community centre today.

a. There were 122 fewer people yesterday. How many people were there yesterday?

_____

b. 102 of the people were at the library yesterday. How many people were not at the library?

**Hints**

Use the answer from Question 10a to find the answer.

_____

⑪ Lyle is solving a 2000-piece puzzle.

a. He has put 451 pieces together. How many pieces are not put together?

_____

b. 89 of the pieces not put together have straight edges. How many of them do not have straight edges?

_____

⑫ The model of a hill is 278 cm tall. The model of a building is 196 cm tall.

    a. How much taller is the hill?

_____

    b. The model of a house is 167 cm shorter than the building. How tall is the house?

_____

⑬

I have an 800-word story to write.

    a. Anita has written 546 words. How many more words are needed?

Anita

_____

    b. Anita finishes her story with 964 words. How many extra words does her story have?

_____

    c. If Anita takes out 96 words, how many words does her story have now?

_____

ISBN: 978-1-77149-201-0

⑭ There were 2142 roses on a farm. 1486 of them were harvested and 156 of them wilted. How many roses are left?

_____

⑮ A cruise ship can carry up to 3600 passengers. The ship has 2498 passengers. How many more passengers can it carry?

_____

⑯ The chart shows the number of male and female athletes that were in the 2004 and 2012 Summer Olympics.

Number of Athletes in the Summer Olympics

Number / Year	Male	Female
2004	6296	4329
2012	5992	4776

　　a. In the 2012 Olympics, how many more male athletes than female athletes were there?

_____

　　b. How many more female athletes were there in the 2012 Olympics than the 2004 Olympics?

_____

　　c. How many fewer male athletes were there in the 2012 Olympics than the 2004 Olympics?

_____

ISBN: 978-1-77149-201-0

Multiplication

solving a variety of word problems that involve multiplication of 1-digit numbers

 **Math Skills**

①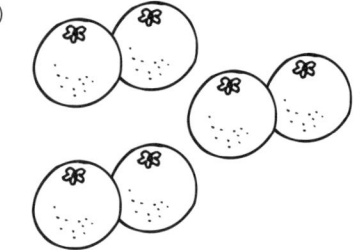

3 × 2 = _____

②

2 × 4 = _____

③

5 × 3 = _____

④

8 × 2 = _____

⑤ 8 × 4 = _____   ⑥ 5 × 7 = _____

⑦ 6 × 1 = _____   ⑧ 9 × 5 = _____

⑨ 4 × 7 = _____   ⑩ 10 × 5 = _____

⑪ 5 × 2 = _____   ⑫ 7 × 6 = _____

⑬ 6 × 3 = _____   ⑭ 10 × 1 = _____

⑮ 9 × 3 = _____   ⑯ 3 × 8 = _____

⑰ 6 × 6 = _____   ⑱ 4 × 4 = _____

⑲ 10 × 3 = _____   ⑳ 9 × 10 = _____

㉑
$$\begin{array}{r} 8 \\ \times\ 6 \\ \hline \end{array}$$
㉒
$$\begin{array}{r} 7 \\ \times\ 7 \\ \hline \end{array}$$
㉓
$$\begin{array}{r} 3 \\ \times\ 7 \\ \hline \end{array}$$

㉔
$$\begin{array}{r} 9 \\ \times\ 6 \\ \hline \end{array}$$
㉕
$$\begin{array}{r} 2 \\ \times\ 9 \\ \hline \end{array}$$
㉖
$$\begin{array}{r} 6 \\ \times\ 4 \\ \hline \end{array}$$

㉗
$$\begin{array}{r} 10 \\ \times\ 4 \\ \hline \end{array}$$
㉘
$$\begin{array}{r} 10 \\ \times\ 7 \\ \hline \end{array}$$
㉙
$$\begin{array}{r} 7 \\ \times\ 9 \\ \hline \end{array}$$

ISBN: 978-1-77149-201-0

Problem Solving

Try This!

Mr. Liam is packaging 3 plums into each bag. He has packaged 4 bags. How many plums has he packaged?

Solution:

Step 1: **Write the number sentence.**

$$3 \times 4 = \boxed{}$$

no. of plums   no. of   total no. of
in a bag   bags   plums

> The order of the numbers in multiplication does not change the answer.

Step 2: **Illustrate the problem to find the answer.**

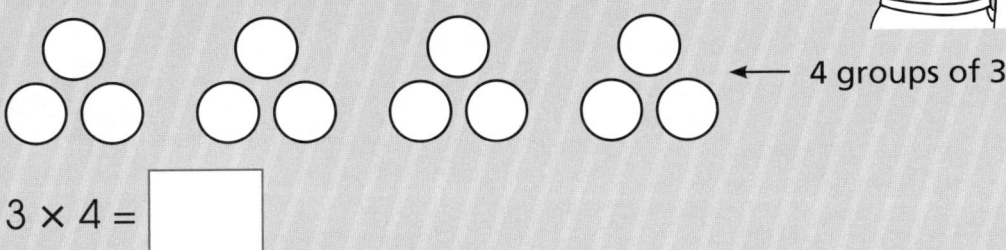

← 4 groups of 3

$$3 \times 4 = \boxed{}$$

Step 3: **Write a concluding sentence.**

Mr. Liam has packaged $\boxed{}$ plums.

① Mr. Liam packaged 5 cabbages into each box. He packaged 3 boxes. How many cabbages did he package altogether?

Mr. Liam packaged _____ cabbages altogether.

ISBN: 978-1-77149-201-0

②

> Tennis balls are sold in cans of 3 at a sports store.

a. If the store sells 7 cans, how many tennis balls are sold?

_____ tennis balls are sold.

b. Tennis racquets are sold in pairs. If 6 pairs are sold, how many racquets are sold?

 **Hints**

A "pair" means a set of two.

_____ racquets are sold.

③ Nancy baked 5 trays of muffins. Each tray holds 9 muffins. How many muffins did she bake?

Nancy baked _____ muffins.

ISBN: 978-1-77149-201-0

④ Isaac built 6 block towers. Each tower is 4 blocks high.

   a. How many blocks did he use in total?

   Isaac used _____ blocks in total.

   b. Brandon built 3 block towers. Each tower is 7 blocks high.
   Who used more blocks for his towers?

   _____ used more blocks.
   Isaac/Brandon

⑤

A carton of juice fills 8 cups.

Will 3 cartons of juice be enough If Alice wants each of her 25 friends to have one cup of juice?

Alice

3 cartons of juice _____ be enough.
will/will not

ISBN: 978-1-77149-201-0

⑥ Mike sold 7 ice cream cones and 4 sundaes.

a. How many scoops of ice cream were sold as cones?

_____

b. How many scoops of ice cream were sold as sundaes?

_____

c. How much money did Mike make by selling cones?

_____

d. How much money did Mike make by selling sundaes?

_____

ISBN: 978-1-77149-201-0

⑦ A banana tree has 6 bananas in each bundle. If it has 9 bundles, how many bananas are there?

_____

⑧ Karla wants to make 6 bracelets. Each one needs 8 beads. How many beads does she need in all?

_____

⑨ Farmer Ben has planted 3 rows of cucumber plants. Each row has 2 cucumber plants.

a. How many cucumber plants are there?

_____

b.

Each cucumber plant produces 6 cucumbers.

How many cucumbers does Farmer Ben have?

Farmer Ben

_____

ISBN: 978-1-77149-201-0

⑩ Crayons are sold in boxes of 10.

   a. Bryan buys a box for himself and a box for his sister. How many crayons do Bryan and his sister have altogether?

   _____

   b. Mrs. Lane buys 4 boxes of crayons for her children. How many crayons do her children have in all?

   _____

⑪ There are 6 softball teams in a league. Each team has 10 players. How many players are there in the league?

   _____

⑫ Patrick bought 3 packets of cookies. Each packet had 10 cookies.

   a. Patrick ate 3 cookies each day. How many cookies were eaten in 5 days?

   _____

   b.

If I ate 4 cookies a day instead, would I have finished all the cookies in 7 days?

Patrick

   _____

ISBN: 978-1-77149-201-0

⑬ Hannah learns 2 French words and 3 Spanish words each day. How many new words will she learn in a week?

_____

⑭ Naomi has soccer practice twice a week. Each practice lesson is 2 hours long.

a. How many hours of practice will she have in 1 week?

_____

b. How many hours of practice will she have in 5 weeks?

_____

⑮ Ms. Carol takes the bus to and from work each day. One bus ride costs $3.

a. How much money will she spend in 5 days?

Ms. Carol

_____

b.  A daily bus pass costs $5. How much do I have to pay for 5 days if I buy the daily bus pass instead?

_____

solving a variety of word problems that involve division of numbers up to 81

 **Math Skills**

①

$10 \div 5 =$ _____

②

$12 \div 4 =$ _____

③

$16 \div 8 =$ _____

④

$18 \div 6 =$ _____

⑤ $4 \overline{)16}$

⑥ $5 \overline{)46}$ R

⑦ $3 \overline{)27}$

⑧ $2 \overline{)11}$ R

⑨ $6 \overline{)24}$

⑩ $7 \overline{)22}$ R

⑪ $56 \div 8 =$ _____

⑫ $24 \div 6 =$ _____

⑬ $15 \div 2 =$ _____

⑭ $42 \div 7 =$ _____

⑮ $64 \div 8 =$ _____

⑯ $37 \div 4 =$ _____

⑰ $44 \div 5 =$ _____

⑱ $28 \div 3 =$ _____

⑲ $63 \div 9 =$ _____

ISBN: 978-1-77149-201-0

 **Problem Solving**

Mindy puts her 6 marbles equally into 3 bags. How many marbles are there in each bag?

Solution:

Step 1: Write a number sentence.

$$6 \div 3 = \boxed{}$$

total no. of marbles   no. of bags   no. of marbles in each bag

> You can also use drawings to help you find the answer.

Step 2: Use its related facts to find the answer.

Think $3 \times ? = 6$

answer

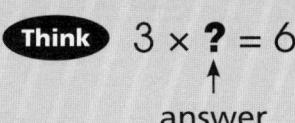

Step 3: Write a concluding sentence.

There are $\boxed{}$ marbles in each bag.

① Nancy has 15 marbles. She puts them equally into 5 bags. How many marbles are there in each bag?

There are _____ marbles in each bag.

ISBN: 978-1-77149-201-0

② Farmer Ken has 30 sheep. He wants 6 sheep in each pen. How many pens does he need?

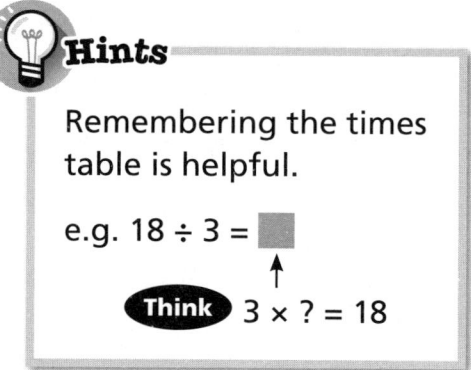

Hints

Remembering the times table is helpful.

e.g. $18 \div 3 = \blacksquare$

Think $3 \times ? = 18$

Farmer Ken needs _____ pens.

③ Winnie used 64 gumdrops to decorate 8 brownies. How many gumdrops did each brownie have?

Each brownie had _____ gumdrops.

④ Tim sorts his rock collection equally into 8 cases. If Tim has 56 rocks, how many rocks should there be in each case?

There should be _____ rocks in each case.

ISBN: 978-1-77149-201-0

⑤ I'm sharing 12 hockey cards with two of my friends equally.

Galvin

a. How many cards will each person get?

Each person will get _____ cards.

b. If Galvin shares the hockey cards with 3 of his friends instead, how many cards will each person get?

Each person will get _____ cards.

⑥ Elaine is reading a 49-page book. If she reads 7 pages each day, will she finish her book in a week?

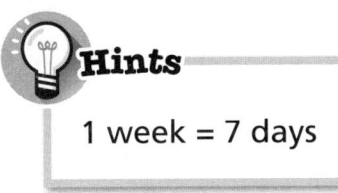

Hints

1 week = 7 days

Elaine _____ finish her book in a week.
        will/will not

ISBN: 978-1-77149-201-0

⑦ It takes Melody 6 minutes to write a holiday card. How many holiday cards will she write in an hour?

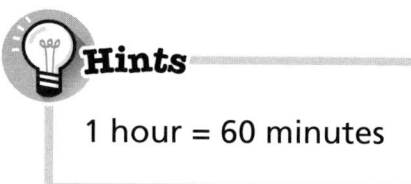

Hints

1 hour = 60 minutes

⑧ Every day, Mr. and Mrs. Lee eat 2 buns each. In how many days will they finish 12 buns?

⑨ Aunt Jenny has 37 buttons. Each shirt needs 5 buttons.

a. How many shirts can Aunt Jenny sew buttons onto?

b. How many buttons remain?

ISBN: 978-1-77149-201-0

⑩ Each table seats 6 guests. There are 26 guests. How many tables are needed to seat all of the guests?

_____

⑪ A box holds 8 muffins. There are 34 muffins that Albert needs to package. How many muffins cannot be packaged?

_____

⑫ Jane and 6 of her friends equally share 24 bottles of water for a hike.

a. How many bottles of water does each person get? How many bottles remain?

_____

b. If another friend joins the hike, can all the bottles of water be divided equally?

_____

ISBN: 978-1-77149-201-0

⑬ Arthur has $20. Each toy car is $3. How many toy cars can he buy at most?

_____

⑭ Edwin is folding his laundry. He folds 24 shirts into stacks of 6.

a. How many shirts are there in each stack?

_____

b. How many stacks will there be if each stack has 8 shirts?

_____

⑮ Chef Lisa is buying packs of spaghetti. She has $17 and each pack of spaghetti costs $2.

a. How many packs of spaghetti can she buy at most?

_____

b.

> If I divide 45 meatballs among 8 plates of pasta, how many meatballs will be left?

Chef Lisa

_____

ISBN: 978-1-77149-201-0

⑯ A science book has 9 chapters. Each chapter has the same number of pages. There are 72 pages in all.

a. How many pages are there in each chapter?

_____

b. It takes Zara 56 minutes to read a chapter. How many minutes does Zara spend reading a page?

_____

c. Leo is reading the same book. He needs 64 minutes to finish a chapter. How many minutes does Leo spend reading a page?

_____

⑰ Ms. Kane groups her class of 26 students into teams of 6.

a. How many teams of 6 are there?

_____

b. If each remaining student is assigned to a team of 6, how many teams will have 7 students?

_____

ISBN: 978-1-77149-201-0

Fractions and Decimals

solving a variety of word problems that involve fractions and decimals

 **Math Skills**

① Write fractions for the shaded parts.

_____   _____   _____

_____   _____

② Colour to show each fraction or decimal. Then put them in order.

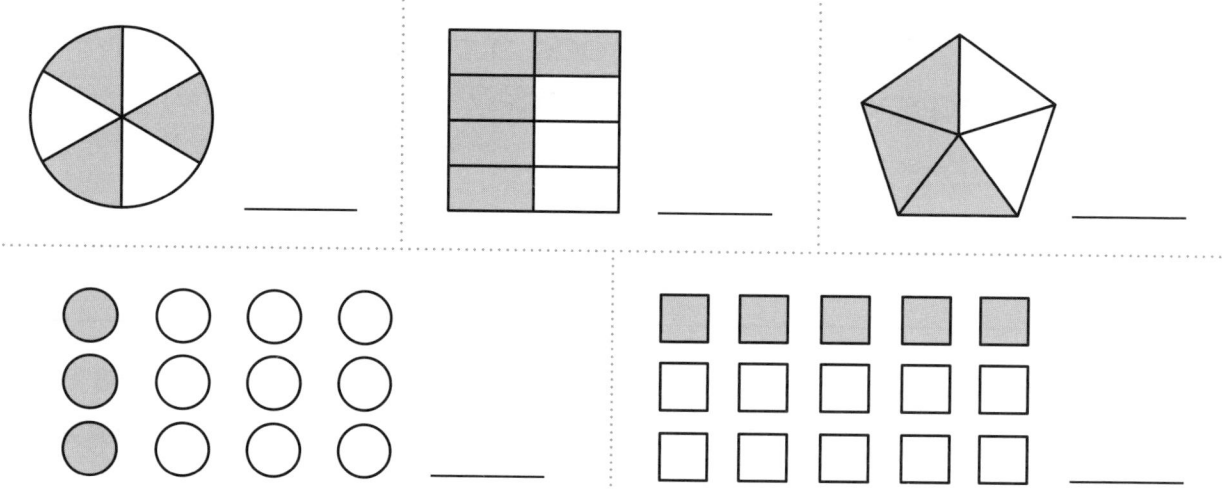

$\frac{2}{5}$

0.8

$\frac{5}{6}$

0.2

Least to Greatest ☐ < ☐ < ☐ < ☐

ISBN: 978-1-77149-201-0

 **Problem Solving**

Try This!

A cake was divided into 8 equal pieces. Kayla ate $\frac{3}{8}$ of the cake. How many pieces did she eat?

Solution:

Step 1: Draw a diagram to show the fraction.

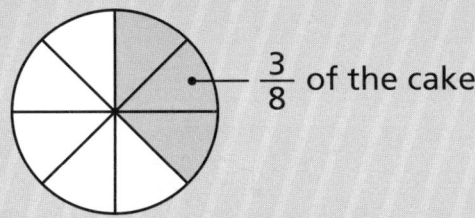 $\frac{3}{8}$ of the cake

It is important that all parts are equal when showing a fraction.

Step 2: Write a concluding sentence.

Kayla ate ☐ pieces.

① Refer to the question above. Kayla's sister, Karen, ate $\frac{1}{8}$ of the cake.

a. How many pieces did Karen eat?

Karen ate _____ piece(s).

b. Kayla's brother, Kyle, ate $\frac{4}{8}$ of the cake. Which child ate the most pieces of cake?

_____ ate the most pieces of cake.

ISBN: 978-1-77149-201-0

②

> This piece of wood is divided into 6 equal squares. 3 squares will be painted red and 1 square will be painted green.

What fraction of the piece of wood will

a. be painted red?

_____ of the piece of wood will be painted red.

b. be painted green?

_____ of the piece of wood will be painted green.

c. not be painted?

_____ of the piece of wood will not be painted.

ISBN: 978-1-77149-201-0

③ Lucy ate $\frac{1}{4}$ of a pie and Bernard ate $\frac{1}{3}$ of it. Who ate more pie?

_____ ate more pie.

④ Mrs. Jones made jelly using $\frac{1}{2}$ cup of sugar and $\frac{1}{6}$ cup of gelatin. Which ingredient did she use more?

Mrs. Jones used more _____ .

⑤ I'll paint $\frac{3}{8}$ of this wall blue and $\frac{3}{5}$ of it pink.

Will Elaine use more or less blue paint than pink paint?

Elaine

Elaine will use _____ blue paint.
<u>more/less</u>

⑥ Arnold has 9 toy cars and Greg has 12 toy cars.

a. 3 toy cars in Arnold's collection are red. What fraction of his collection is red?

_____

b. $\frac{1}{6}$ of Greg's toy cars are red. How many red toy cars does Greg have?

_____

c. Arnold has 6 blue toy cars. What fraction of Arnold's collection is blue?

_____

d. $\frac{1}{3}$ of Greg's toy cars are blue. Who has more blue toy cars?

_____

ISBN: 978-1-77149-201-0

⑦ Caleb's birthday cake was cut into 10 equal slices.

a. 0.6 of the cake was eaten. How many slices were eaten?

_____

b. Caleb ate 2 slices. How much of the cake did Caleb eat in decimals?

_____

⑧ There were 10 slices of bread in a loaf.

a. 0.2 of the loaf was used to make French toast. How many slices were used?

_____

b. I used 5 slices to make this sandwich. How much of the loaf did I use in decimals?

Amy

_____

ISBN: 978-1-77149-201-0

⑨

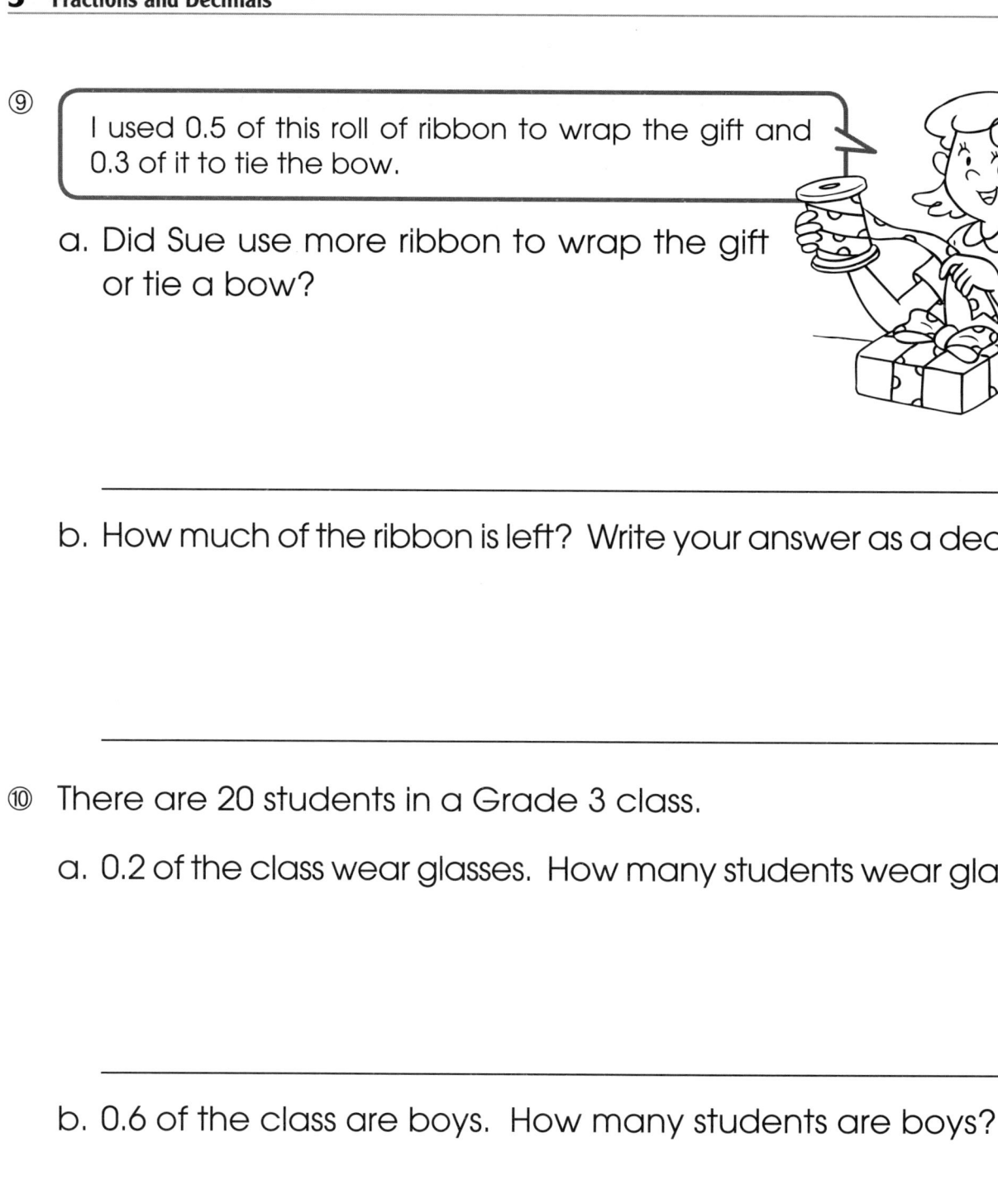

I used 0.5 of this roll of ribbon to wrap the gift and 0.3 of it to tie the bow.

a. Did Sue use more ribbon to wrap the gift or tie a bow?

_____

b. How much of the ribbon is left? Write your answer as a decimal.

_____

⑩ There are 20 students in a Grade 3 class.

a. 0.2 of the class wear glasses. How many students wear glasses?

_____

b. 0.6 of the class are boys. How many students are boys?

_____

c. 10 students go to school by school bus. How much of the class goes to school by school bus in decimals?

_____

ISBN: 978-1-77149-201-0

⑪ Emily ordered a pepperoni pizza and a Hawaiian pizza. Each pizza was cut into 10 equal slices.

a. $\frac{7}{10}$ of the pepperoni pizza and $\frac{5}{10}$ of the Hawaiian pizza were eaten. Which pizza has fewer slices left? How many slices fewer?

_____

b. How much of the pepperoni pizza was eaten in decimals?

_____

c. Emily says, "$1\frac{1}{2}$ of the pizzas were eaten." Is she correct?

_____

⑫ Mr. Richards, the caretaker of an office, needs to replace 20 light bulbs. The light bulbs come in packs of 6.

a. If Mr. Richards has $2\frac{2}{6}$ boxes of light bulbs, does he have enough?

_____

b.

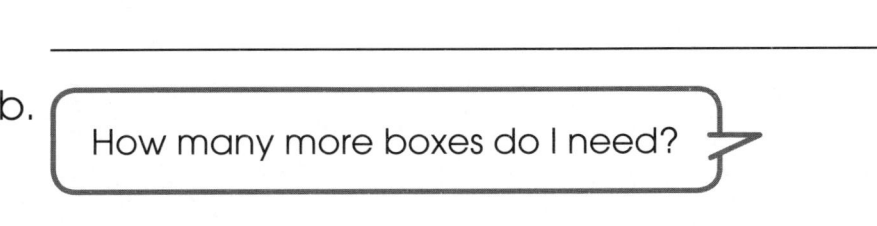
How many more boxes do I need?

Mr. Richards

_____

ISBN: 978-1-77149-201-0

Money

Math Skills

① Find the money amounts and write them in 2 ways.

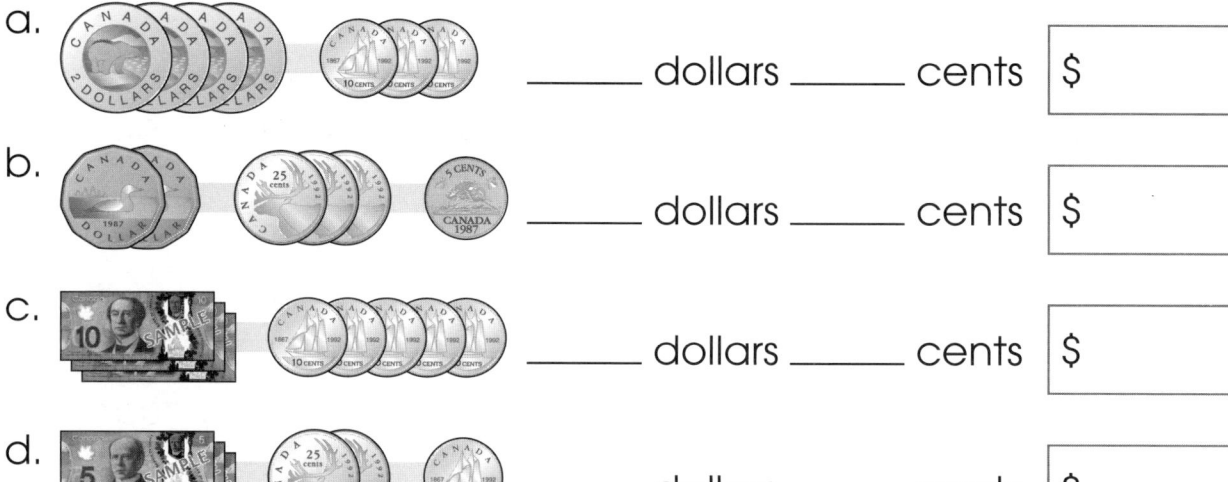

a. _____ dollars _____ cents $ [ ]

b. _____ dollars _____ cents $ [ ]

c. _____ dollars _____ cents $ [ ]

d. _____ dollars _____ cents $ [ ]

② Check the fewest bills and coins needed to pay for each toy.

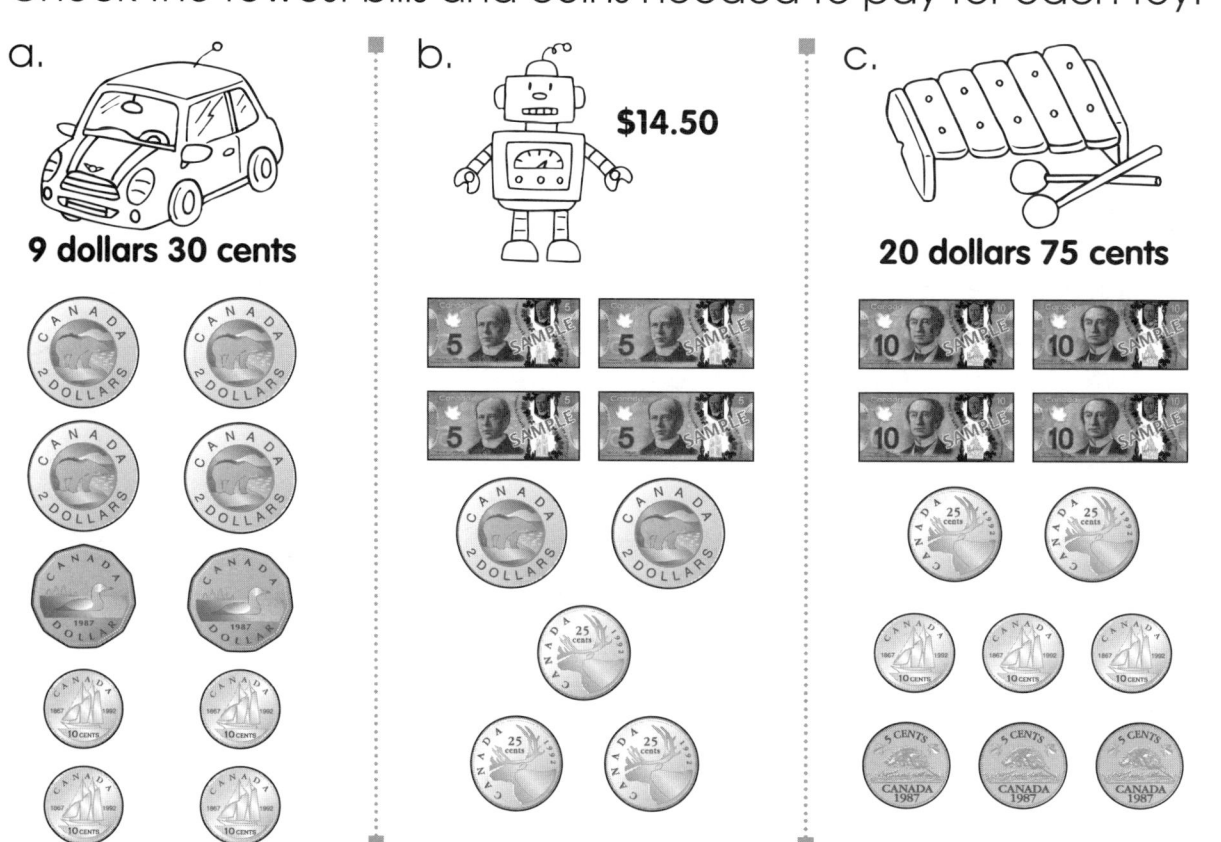

a.

9 dollars 30 cents

b.

$14.50

c.

20 dollars 75 cents

ISBN: 978-1-77149-201-0

 **Problem Solving**

A shirt costs $12.25. How much do 2 shirts cost?

Solution:

Step 1: **Rewrite the decimal as dollars and cents.**

$12.25 = ☐ dollars ☐ cents

Step 2: **Add to find the total.**

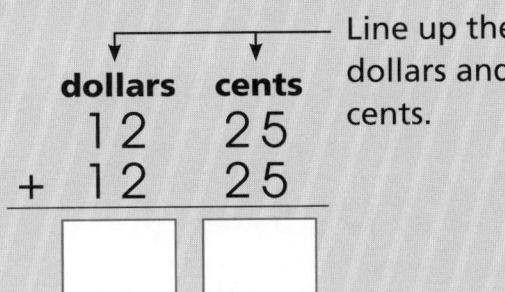

Line up the dollars and cents.

dollars	cents
1 2	2 5
+ 1 2	2 5
☐	☐

Sometimes, you may need to trade 100 cents for 1 dollar.

e.g.

	dollars	cents
	1	50
+	1	60
	3 ²~~2~~	~~110~~ 10

Total: $3.10

Step 3: **Write a concluding sentence.**

2 shirts cost $ ☐ .

① Janice had $6.50. She has earned $4.75 from chores. How much money does she have now?

Janice has $_____ now.

ISBN: 978-1-77149-201-0

② Hugh has $3.75. Paul has $0.80 more than Hugh.

a. How much does Paul have?

Paul has $_____ .

b. How much do the boys have in all?

The boys have $_____ in all.

c.

I have $4.55 more than Paul.

How much does Sally have?

Sally

Sally has $_____ .

ISBN: 978-1-77149-201-0

③ A bottle of juice costs $3.80. A can of juice costs $1.75. How much more does a bottle of juice cost than a can of juice?

A bottle of juice costs $_____ more than a can of juice.

④ Heather saved $8.10 last week and $5.85 this week. How much more did Heather save last week?

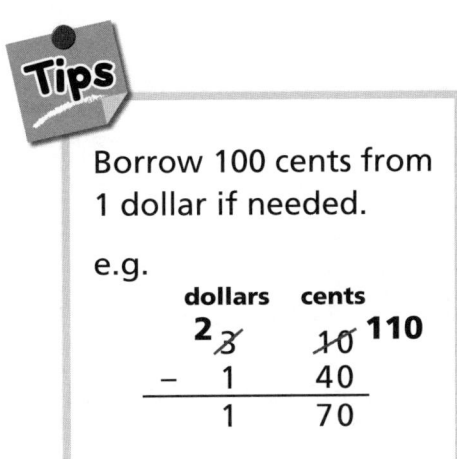

Borrow 100 cents from 1 dollar if needed.

e.g.

	dollars	cents
	2 $\cancel{3}$	$\cancel{10}$ **110**
−	1	40
	1	70

Heather saved $_____ more last week.

⑤ Store A sells a box of cereal at $4.95. Store B sells it at $4.70. Which store offers a better price and by how much less?

_____ offers a better price by $_____ less.

ISBN: 978-1-77149-201-0

⑥ A binder costs $3.15.

   a. Fred wants to buy 2 binders. How much will it cost?

_____

   b. Fred pays $10 for the binders. What will his change be?

_____

⑦ A box of crayons cost $10.70. Alexa had a $2.50 off coupon.

   a. How much did the box of crayons cost with the coupon?

_____

   b.
> I bought the box of crayons and got $11.80 in change. How much did I pay?

Alexa

_____

ISBN: 978-1-77149-201-0

⑧ The menu shows the prices of the food items.

Chef Burger	
Beef Burger	$5.95
Chicken Burger	$5.85
Fish Burger	$6.05
Drink	$2.05
Cookie	$1.50

Get $2 off when you buy a burger, a drink, and a cookie.

a. Tessa buys a beef burger and a drink. How much do they cost in total?

_____

b. Francis buys 2 fish burgers. What is the total cost?

_____

c. How much more does it cost to buy a fish burger than a chicken burger?

_____

d.
> I bought a fish burger, a drink, and a cookie. How much did they cost in total?

_____

ISBN: 978-1-77149-201-0

⑨ Karl paid with a $5 bill for a bottle of apple juice that cost $2.10. What was his change?

_____

⑩ Esther paid with 2 toonies for a box of pencils. She got $0.55 in change. How much did the box of pencils cost?

_____

⑪ Jim bought a $7.85 toy car and got 1 toonie, 1 dime, and 1 nickel in change. How much did Jim pay?

_____

⑫ Amy has 1 toonie, 1 loonie, and 1 quarter. A doll costs $4.50.

a. How much more does she need to buy the doll?

_____

b. Amy's sister gives 1 toonie to Amy. Does Amy have enough money to buy the doll now? If so, how much will she have left?

_____

ISBN: 978-1-77149-201-0

⑬

> I bought 2 cans of soup with a $10 bill.

Joshua

a. If each can cost $2.60, how much did Joshua spend in all?

_____

b. Joshua got back $3.80 in change. Did he get the correct amount of change? If not, what should his change be?

_____

c. What should Joshua's change be in the fewest bills and coins?

_____

⑭ Diane paid with a $10 bill for boxes of oatmeal and now she has 2 toonies and 2 dimes in change.

a. A box of oatmeal cost $2.90. How many boxes did she buy?

_____

b. What will Diane's change be with the fewest bills and coins if she buys 3 boxes instead?

_____

ISBN: 978-1-77149-201-0

Time and Temperature

solving a variety of word problems that involve time and temperature

 **Math Skills**

① Write each time in two ways.

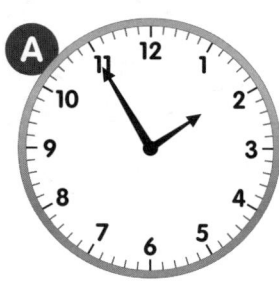

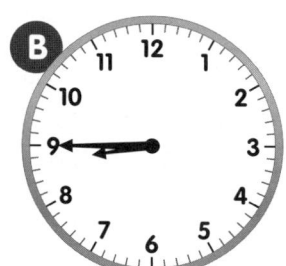

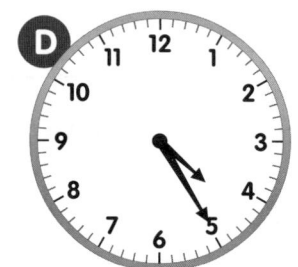

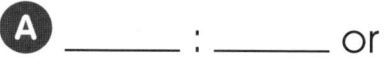

A _____ : _____ or

_____ minutes before _____

B _____ or

_____

C _____ or

_____

D _____ or

_____

② Record the temperatures and match the thermometers with the drinks.

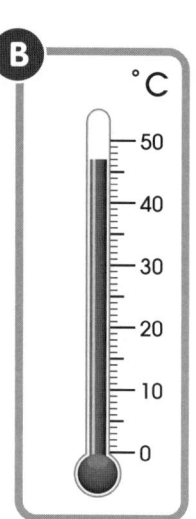

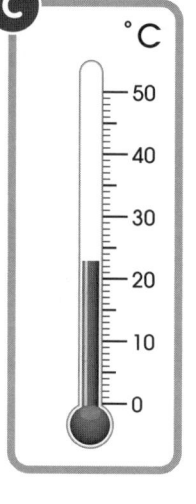

_____ °C   _____   _____

ISBN: 978-1-77149-201-0

 **Problem Solving**

A show starts at 4:00 and ends at 5:00. How long is the show in minutes?

Solution:

Step 1: **Consider the times on the clocks.**

It takes 1 h for the hour hand (the shorter hand) to move from 4:00 to 5:00.

Step 2: **Find the elapsed time.**

Elapsed time: ☐ h

1 h = 60 min

Step 3: **Write a concluding sentence.**

The show is ☐ minutes long.

① Ezra started hiking at 6:15 and finished at 8:15. How many hours did he hike for? Draw the times on the clocks to help you.

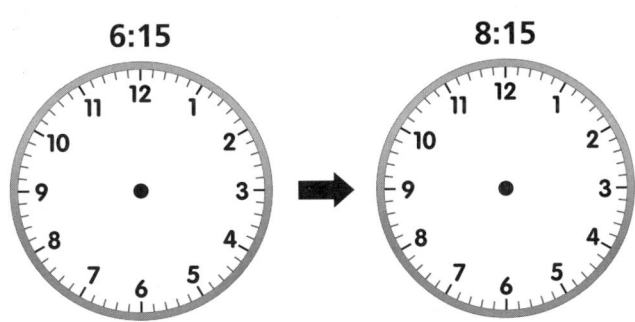

Ezra hiked for _____ hours.

ISBN: 978-1-77149-201-0

②   Natalie leaves for school at 7:30 and arrives at 8:10.

     a. How many minutes does it take her to get to school?

        It takes Natalie _____ minutes to get to school.

     b. School starts at 8:35. By how many minutes early is Natalie?

        Natalie is _____ minutes early.

③   Mr. Smith baked a cake. He started at 11:45 a.m. and finished at 1:15 p.m. How long was the cake baked for?

Hints

"a.m." means before noon; "p.m." means after noon.

The cake was baked for _____ h _____ min.

ISBN: 978-1-77149-201-0

④ Here is Nancy's calendar.

a. Draw to mark the days on her calendar.

| February 2017 |||||||
Sun	Mon	Tue	Wed	Thu	Fri	Sat
			1	2	3	4
5	6	7	8	9	10	11
12	13	14	15	16	17	18
19	20	21	22	23	24	25
26	27	28				

Days

Groundhog Day
February 2

Valentine's Day
February 14

Family Day
February 20

Nancy

b.

My birthday is 2 days after Groundhog Day.

When is Nancy's birthday?

_____

c. Nancy has a test a week after Valentine's Day. When is the test?

_____

d. Nancy's family will be away for a trip from February 16 to February 20. How long is the trip?

_____

⑤ On a winter morning, Sue measured the temperatures of different places with a thermometer.

a. Record the temperatures. Match the thermometers with the places.

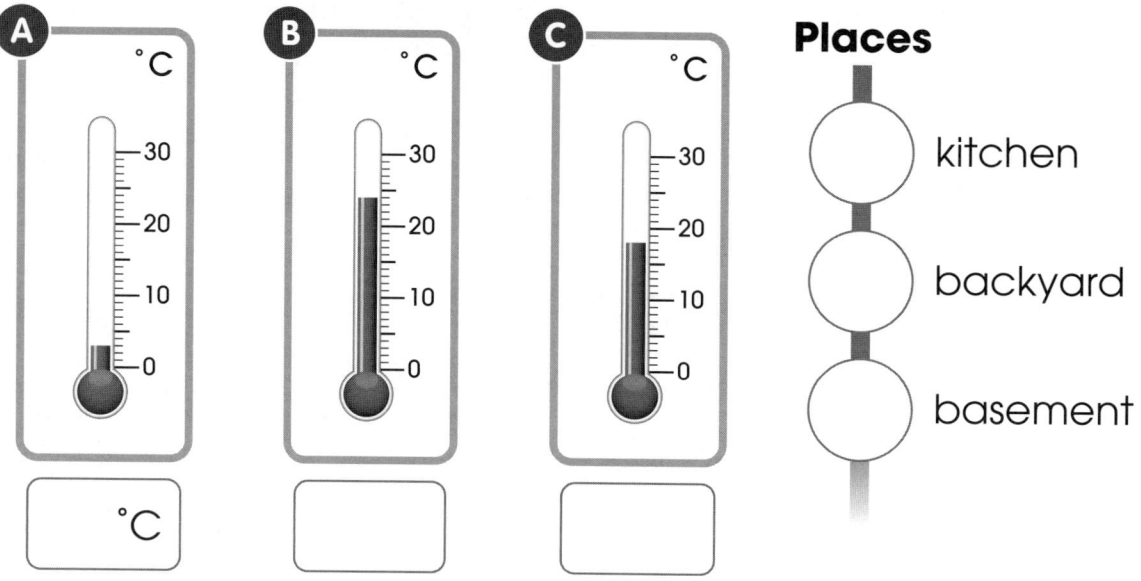

b. Which place had the highest temperature?

_____

c. Which place had the lowest temperature?

_____

d. In the afternoon, the temperature in the backyard rose to 11°C. By how many °C did the temperature rise?

_____

e. In the evening, the temperature had dropped 8°C since the afternoon. What was the temperature in the evening? Show it on the thermometer.

_____

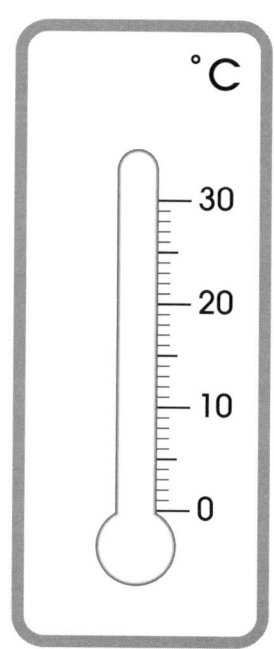

ISBN: 978-1-77149-201-0

⑥ The school nurse has taken the temperature of some sick students. Having a body temperature of 38°C or greater indicates a fever.

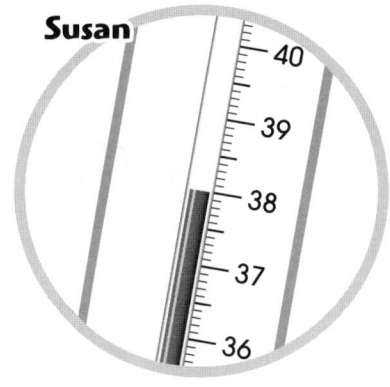

Susan

a. Record the temperature of each student. Does he or she have a fever?

- Susan

_____

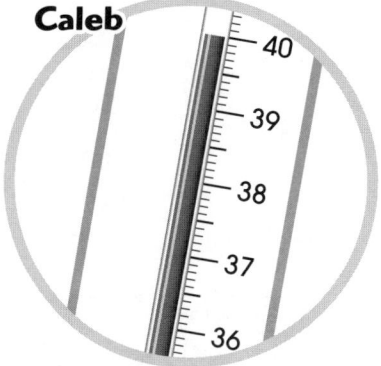

Caleb

- Caleb

_____

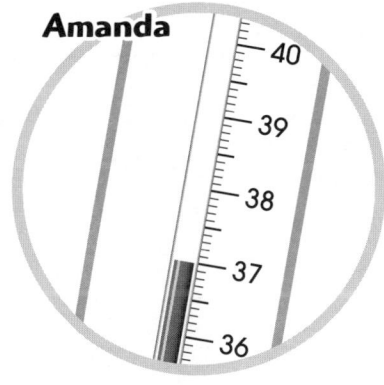

Amanda

- Amanda

_____

b.

A child needs to see a doctor if his or her body temperature is 40°C or greater. Who needs to see a doctor?

_____

⑦ Conrad measured the temperature of a pot of water at 4 different times using a thermometer.

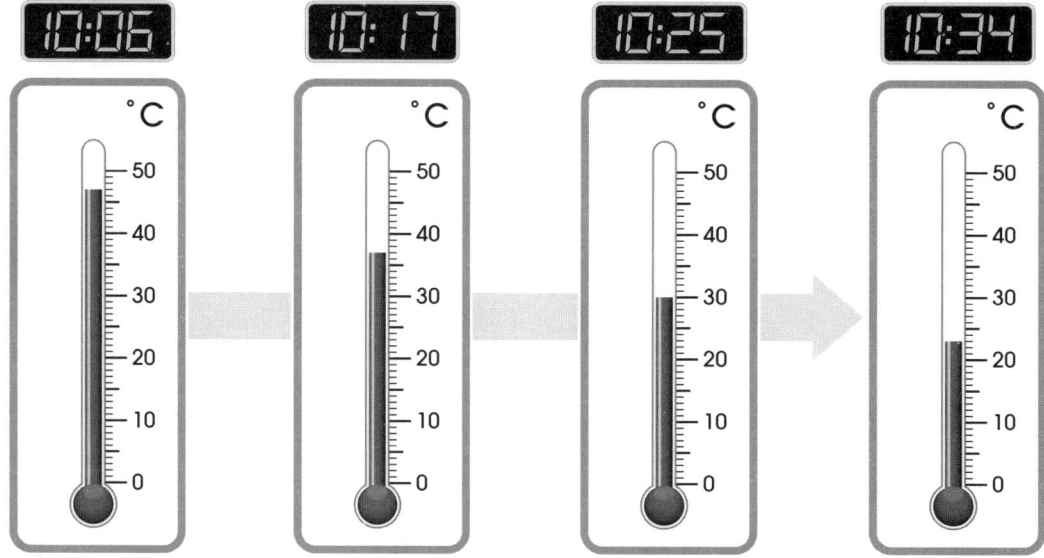

a. Was the pot of water cooling down or warming up? How do you know?

_____

b. Where do you think the pot of water was, on a heated stove or on a table?

**Hints**

Room temperature is about 22°C.

_____

c. How long did it take for the temperature of the water to drop from 37°C to 30°C?

_____

d. How long did it take for the temperature of the water to drop from 47°C to 23°C?

_____

e. What might the temperature of the water be at 10:11?

_____

ISBN: 978-1-77149-201-0

⑧ Jacob took the temperatures throughout the day.

9:00 a.m.

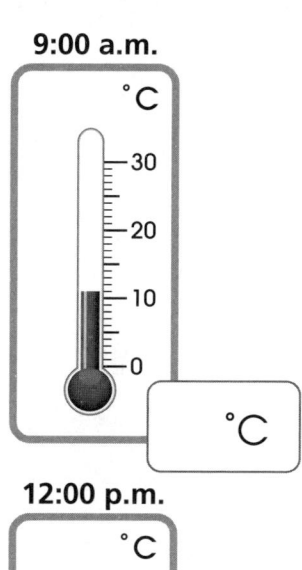

°C

12:00 p.m.

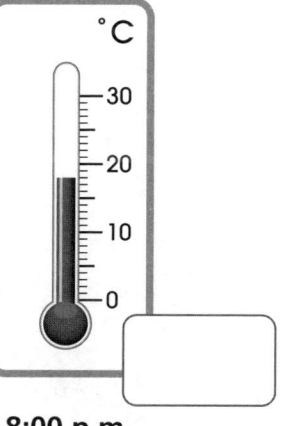

5:45 p.m.

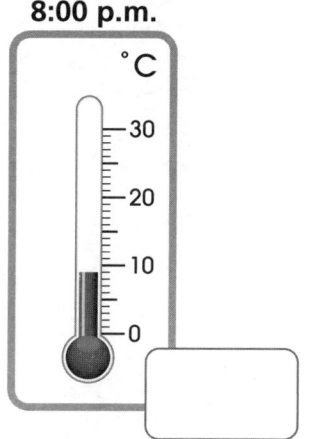

8:00 p.m.

a. What was the temperature change from noon to 5:45 p.m.?

_____

b. How long did it take for the temperature to drop from 27°C to 9°C?

_____

c. Between which time period was there a change of 16°C? How long did it take for the change?

_____

d. Jacob said, "It took 2 hours and 15 minutes for a drop of 9°C." Which time period was Jacob referring to?

_____

e. What was the change in temperature from noon to 8:00 p.m.? How many hours did it take?

_____

ISBN: 978-1-77149-201-0

Capacity and Mass

8

solving a variety of word problems that involve standard units of capacity and mass

Math Skills

Capacity

① Circle the better unit to measure the capacity of each container.

a. cup   mL / L

b. bathtub   mL / L

c. spoon   mL / L

d. pail   mL / L

e. can   mL / L

Mass

③ Circle the better unit to measure the mass of each object.

a. shirt   g / kg

b. desk   g / kg

c. cell phone g / kg

d. car   g / kg

e. apple   g / kg

② Do the matching.

◯ 10 L   ◯ 250 mL

◯ 2 L   ◯ 700 mL

④ Do the matching.

◯ 1 kg   ◯ 6 kg

◯ 230 g   ◯ 4 g

ISBN: 978-1-77149-201-0

 **Problem Solving**

 **Try This!**

Jake's bottle can hold 750 mL of water. Janice's bottle can hold 1 L of water. Whose bottle can hold more?

Solution:

Step 1: Compare the capacities in the same unit.

Jake's bottle: 750 mL

Janice's bottle: 1 L = 1000 mL

Step 2: Write a concluding sentence.

[   ] 's bottle can hold more.

There are 1000 mL in 1 L.

1 L = 1000 mL

① Sink A has a capacity of 1580 mL. Sink B has a capacity of 1 L. Which sink has a greater capacity?

Sink _____ has a greater capacity.

② A red pail can hold 4 L of sand. A green pail can hold 3000 mL of sand. Which pail holds less sand?

The _____ pail holds less sand.

ISBN: 978-1-77149-201-0

③

A jug holds 2 L of water.

a. What is the capacity of 2 jugs in litres?

The capacity is _____ L.

b. What is the capacity of 3 jugs in millilitres?

Hints

Convert from "L" to "mL".

The capacity is _____ mL.

c. How many millilitres of water is there in half of a jug?

There is _____ mL of water.

d. If there is 500 mL of water left in the jug, will it be enough to fill a 1-L bottle?

It _____ be enough to fill a 1-L bottle.
<u>will/will not</u>

ISBN: 978-1-77149-201-0

④ There are three pails – yellow, blue, and red.

a. Colour the pails with the given descriptions.

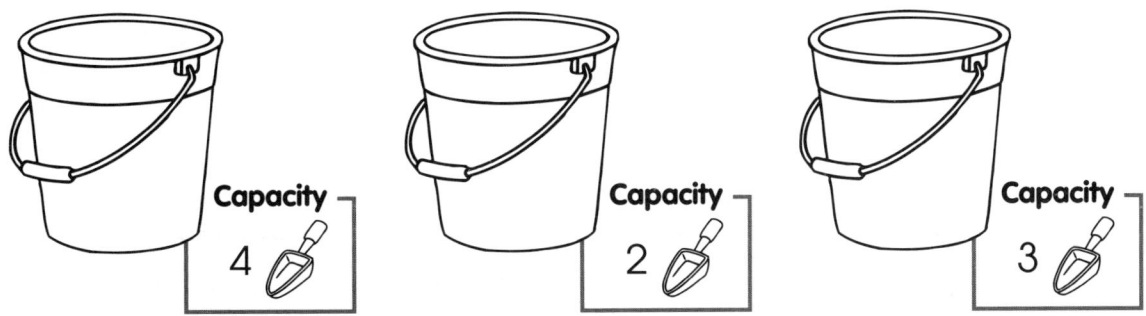

Capacity	Capacity	Capacity
4	2	3

- The red pail has the greatest capacity.
- The yellow pail has half the capacity of the red pail.

> The capacity of the red pail is 4 L.

b. What is the capacity of the yellow pail in litres?

The capacity is _____ L.

c. What is the capacity of the blue pail in millilitres?

The capacity is _____ mL.

d. What is the total capacity of the pails?

The total capacity is _____ L.

ISBN: 978-1-77149-201-0

⑤ Baby Theo is 3 kg and Baby Tina is 2850 g. Who is heavier?

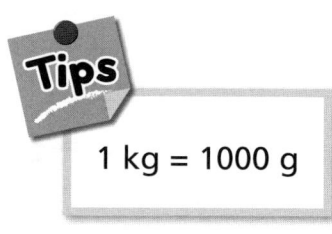

Tips

1 kg = 1000 g

⑥ A toy train is 1974 g and a toy truck is 2 kg. Which toy is lighter?

⑦ Jill bought 2 desserts that weighed 2 kg and 3300 g. If the cake was lighter than the apple pie, what was the weight of the cake in grams?

⑧ A pineapple weighs 3 kg. A squash weighs 5000 g. Do two pineapples of the same weight weigh more or less than one squash?

ISBN: 978-1-77149-201-0

⑨ Farmer Ben puts the following fruits on two scales: 1 watermelon, 3 honeydews, 1 cantaloupe, and 2 papayas.

a. The watermelon weighs 9 kg. What is the weight of 1 honeydew in grams if they are the same weight?

_____

b. A papaya weighs 500 g. What is the weight of 1 cantaloupe in kilograms?

_____

c. How many cantaloupes of the same weight are needed to balance 1 honeydew?

_____

d. How many papayas of the same weight are needed to balance 1 honeydew?

_____

ISBN: 978-1-77149-201-0

⑩ A carton has 2 L of juice. A bottle has a capacity of 1 L.

   a. How many bottles can a carton of juice fill?

_____

   b. A bottle can fill 4 cups. How many cups can a carton of juice fill?

_____

   c. An empty bottle weighs 58 g and an empty cup weighs 90 g. How much heavier is the cup than the bottle?

_____

⑪ A red bucket weighs 180 g and a green bucket weighs 150 g. They both have a capacity of 10 L.

   a. A roof is leaking water. Mike uses the heavier bucket to catch the dripping water because he thinks it can hold more. Is his thinking correct? Explain.

_____

   b. The red bucket is half full after an hour. How much water is there in the bucket in litres?

_____

ISBN: 978-1-77149-201-0

⑫ Cooking Pan A weighs 1 kg and it has a capacity of 750 mL. Cooking Pan B weighs 800 g and it has a capacity of 1 L.

a. Mr. Noah bought the cooking pan that is lighter. Which one did he buy?

_____

b. Ms. Lee bought the cooking pan that has a greater capacity. Which one did she buy?

_____

c. Mrs. Smith ordered both cooking pans online. What is the total weight of the shipment in grams?

_____

⑬ Carl weighs an empty glass jug on a scale.

a. What is the capacity of 2 jugs in millilitres?

_____

b. What is the weight of 3 jugs in grams?

_____

ISBN: 978-1-77149-201-0

Perimeter and Area

solving a variety of word problems that involve finding perimeter and area

 **Math Skills**

①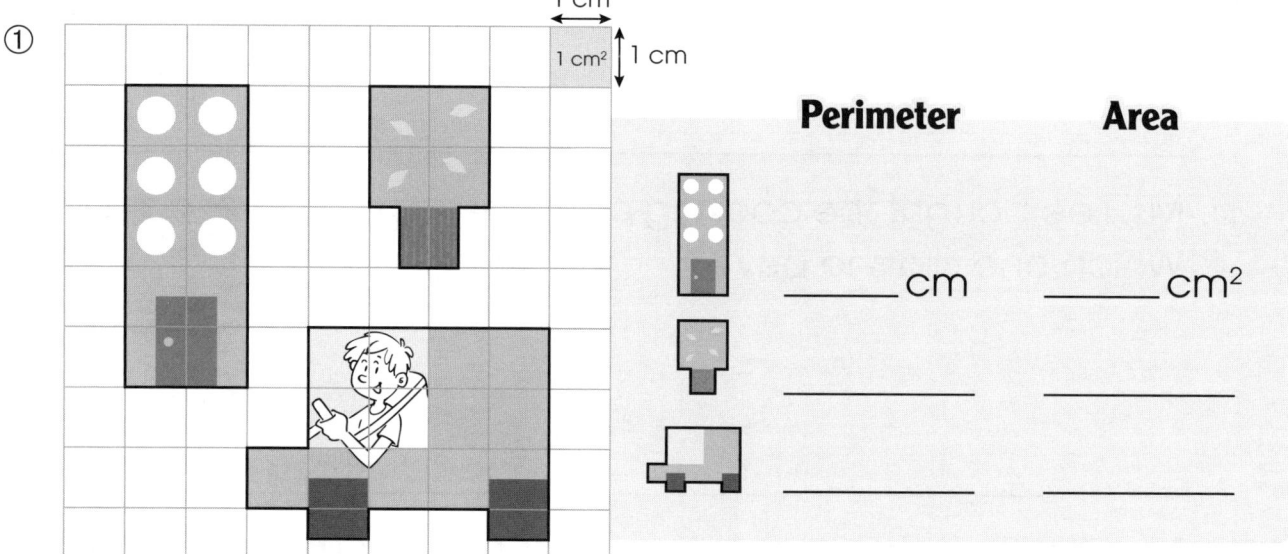

	Perimeter	Area
	_____ cm	_____ cm²
	_____	_____
	_____	_____

②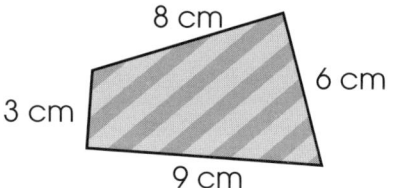

8 cm · 6 cm · 3 cm · 9 cm

Perimeter:

_____ + _____ + _____ + _____

= _____ (cm)

③

2 cm · 2 cm · 3 cm · 5 cm · 3 cm · 5 cm

Perimeter:

_____

= _____

④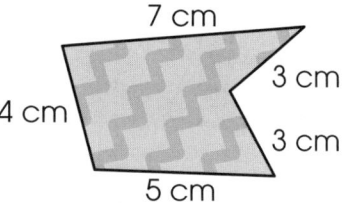

7 cm · 3 cm · 4 cm · 3 cm · 5 cm

Perimeter:

_____

= _____

⑤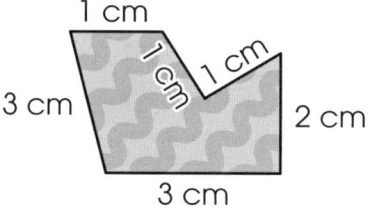

1 cm · 1 cm · 1 cm · 3 cm · 2 cm · 3 cm

Perimeter:

_____

= _____

ISBN: 978-1-77149-201-0

 **Problem Solving**

Try This!

Julie made a coaster. She added a border around it. How long was the border?

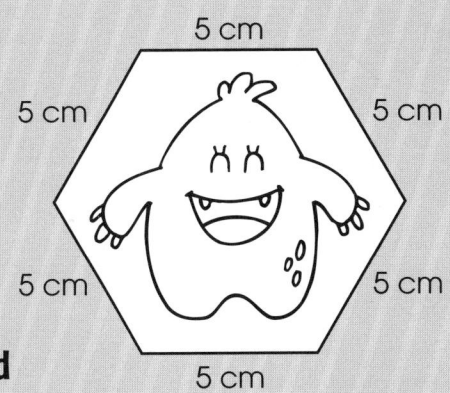

5 cm

5 cm   5 cm

5 cm   5 cm

5 cm

Solution:

Step 1: Add the lengths of the 6 sides to find the perimeter.

$5 + 5 + 5 + 5 + 5 + 5 =$ ☐

Step 2: Write a concluding sentence.

The border was ☐ cm long.

① Julie made 2 more coasters and she added a border around each one. How long were the borders?

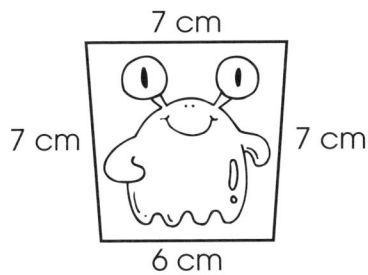

7 cm

7 cm   7 cm

6 cm

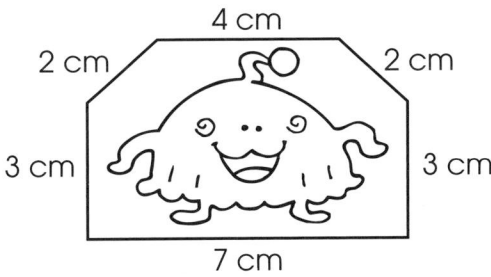

4 cm

2 cm   2 cm

3 cm   3 cm

7 cm

The borders were _____ cm and _____ cm long.

ISBN: 978-1-77149-201-0

② Wesley has drawn a rocket with different shapes. He wants to glue a string around the edges of the shapes. Use a ruler to find out how many centimetres of string each shape needs.

a.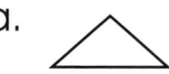

This shape needs _____ cm.

b.

This shape needs _____ cm.

c.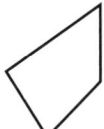

This shape needs _____ cm.

d.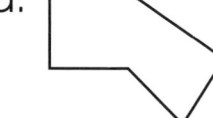

This shape needs _____ cm.

ISBN: 978-1-77149-201-0

③ Phoebe's musical triangle has lengths of 10 cm, 8 cm, and 8 cm. What is the perimeter of the triangle?

The perimeter of the triangle is _____ cm.

④ Oscar made a rectangular poster. It has a length of 30 cm and a width of 20 cm. What is the perimeter of the poster?

Hints
Make a sketch of the poster's shape. Label the sides with the measurements.

The perimeter of the poster is _____ cm.

⑤ Farmer Ken wants to make a pig pen. It is a square that has a side length of 10 m. If he wants to add fencing around the pen, how many metres of fencing does he need?

Hints
The 4 sides of a square have the same length.

Farmer Ken needs _____ m of fencing.

ISBN: 978-1-77149-201-0

⑥ Joshua completed a puzzle. Find the area of each puzzle piece.

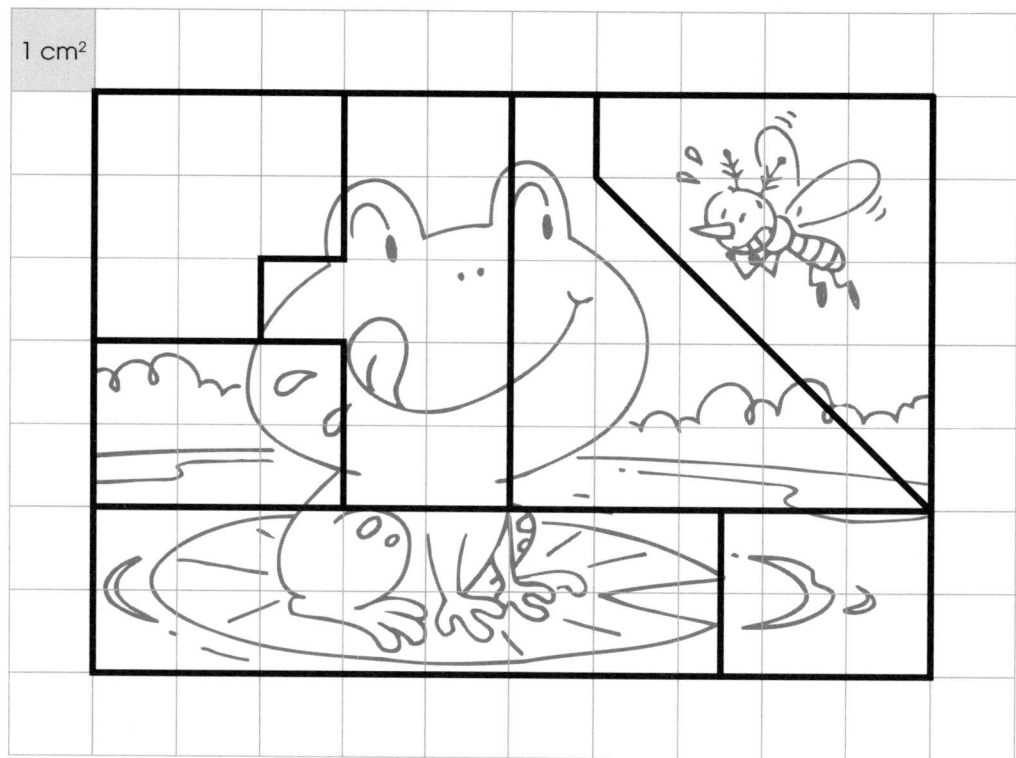

1 cm²

a. **Area**

_____ cm²

_____

_____

_____

_____

_____

_____

b. What is the area of the largest puzzle piece?

_____

c. What is the area of the smallest puzzle piece?

_____

d. What is the area of the puzzle?

_____

ISBN: 978-1-77149-201-0

⑦ Look at the map of Mr. Lee's and Mr. Smith's houses.

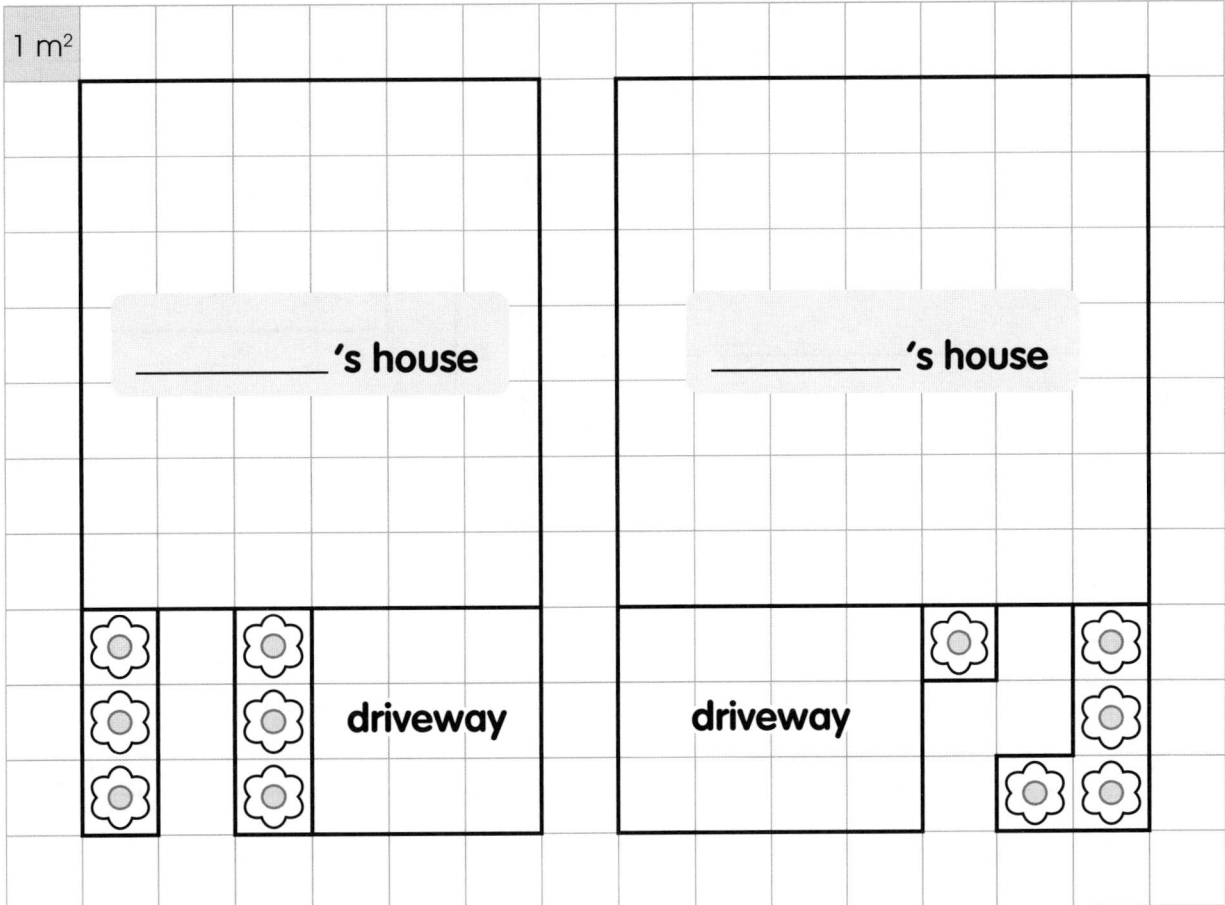

a. Mr. Lee's house covers 49 m² of land. Mr. Smith's house covers 42 m² of land. Label their houses on the map.

b. Whose flower garden covers a greater area? By how much?

_____

c. Whose driveway covers less area? By how much?

_____

ISBN: 978-1-77149-201-0

⑧ The map of Mr. Lee's backyard is shown on the right.

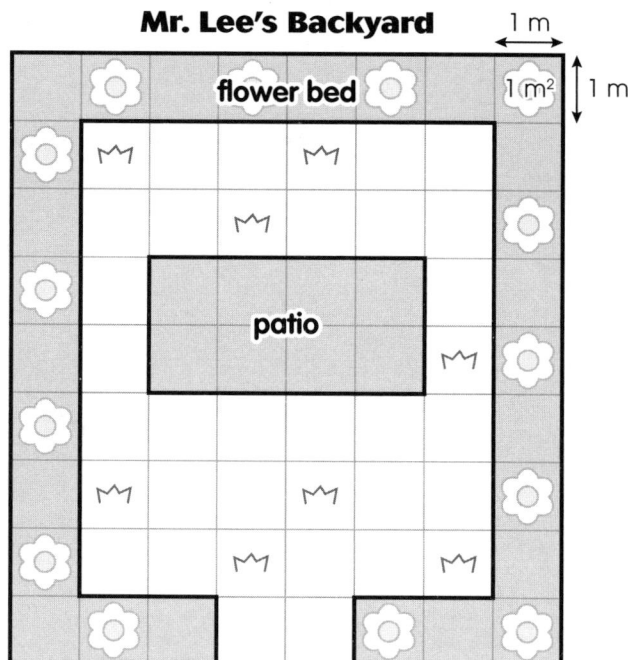

Mr. Lee's Backyard

a. What is the area of the flower bed?

_____

b. Mr. Lee wants to add fencing all around the flower bed. How many metres of fencing does he need?

_____

c. What are the perimeter and the area of the patio?

_____

d. Mr. Lee wants to expand the patio so that it is 1 m away from the flower bed on all sides. What are the perimeter and the area after the expansion?

_____

e. By how much will the area of the lawn decrease after the expansion?

_____

ISBN: 978-1-77149-201-0

⑨ Molly drew a shape on a centimetre grid.

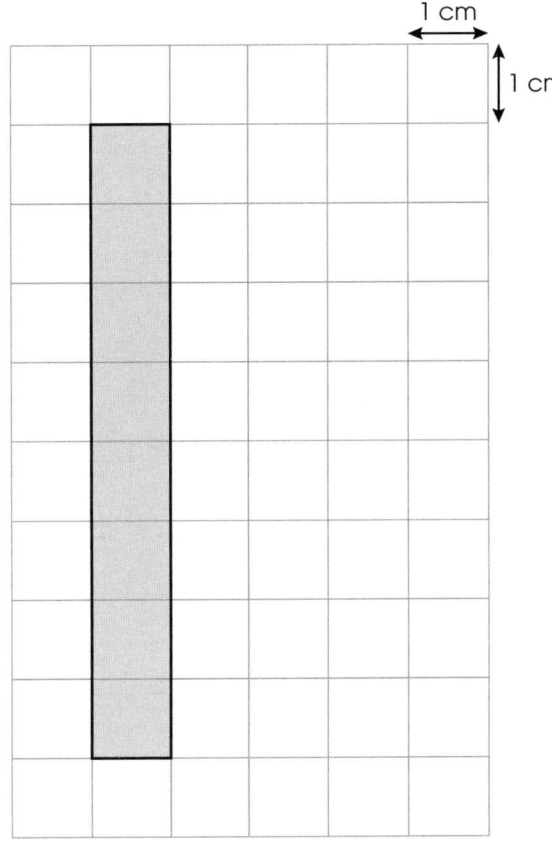

a. What are the perimeter and the area of the shape?

_____

b. Molly wants to draw a different rectangle that has the same area. Draw the shape. What is its perimeter?

_____

⑩ Eric's bedroom has a length of 6 m. Its width is half of its length.

a. What is the width of Eric's bedroom?

_____

b. What is the perimeter of Eric's bedroom?

_____

c. What is the area of Eric's bedroom in square metres?

**Hints**

Make a sketch of the bedroom to find the area.

_____

ISBN: 978-1-77149-201-0

Shapes and Solids

solving a variety of word problems that involve the properties of shapes and solids

Math Skills

Write the names of the shapes and solids.

Shapes

parallelogram   trapezoid

rhombus   kite   triangle

A _____

B _____

C _____

D _____

E _____

Solids

rectangular pyramid   triangular prism

cylinder   sphere   rectangular prism

V _____

W _____

X _____

Y _____

Z _____

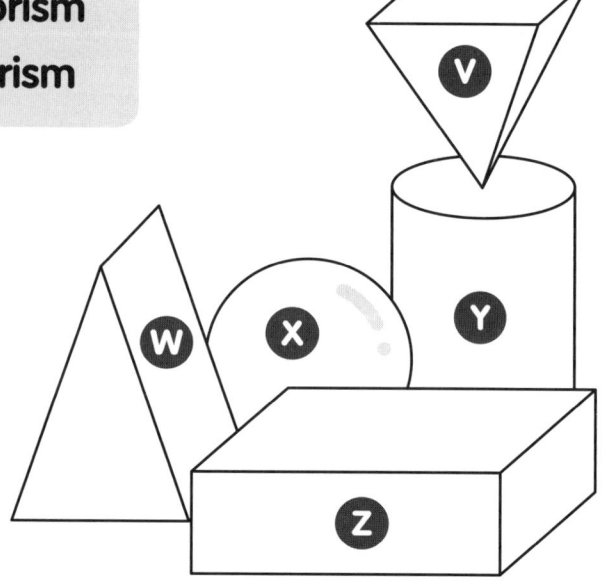

ISBN: 978-1-77149-201-0

 **Problem Solving**

James drew a triangle and a trapezoid. He cut out the one that has 3 vertices. Which one did he cut out?

Solution:

Step 1: Draw the shapes.

triangle   trapezoid

A "vertex" is a corner of a shape. "Vertices" is the plural form of vertex.

Step 2: Circle and count the vertices.

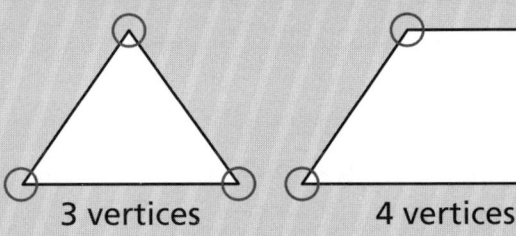

3 vertices   4 vertices

Step 3: Write a concluding sentence.

James cut out the ☐ .

① Karen made a shape using 4 sticks of the same length. If it was not a square, what shape was it?

Tips

Use the shapes shown on page 80 to help you if needed.

It was a _____ .

② Mindy is comparing some shapes that have 4 sides.

    a. "This shape has only 1 pair of sides that have the same length," Mindy says. Draw and name the shape.

        The shape is a _____ .

    b. Mindy is comparing a square and a rhombus. Compare the number of lines of symmetry that each shape has.

        A square has _____ lines of symmetry than a rhombus.
                    more/fewer

    c.

This shape has no line of symmetry.

Draw it out. Then name it if you can.

Mindy

_____

ISBN: 978-1-77149-201-0

③ Joe had 2 long straws and 2 short straws.

a. He made a shape using all 4 straws. It has exactly 1 line of symmetry. What shape did he make?

Joe made a _____ .

b. If Joe makes another shape using 3 of the straws, what shape does he make? How many lines of symmetry does this shape have?

Joe makes a _____ . It has _____ line(s) of symmetry.

c.

> I cut one of the long straws into 2 equal pieces. So, now I have 5 straws.

Joe makes a shape using all of the straws. What shape does he make? How many vertices does it have?

Joe

He makes a _____ . It has _____ vertices.

ISBN: 978-1-77149-201-0

④ Eric has a collection of solids.

Eric's Solids

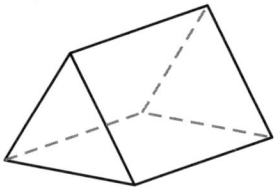

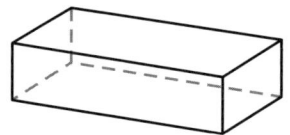

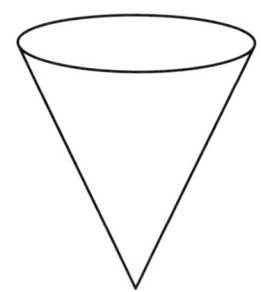

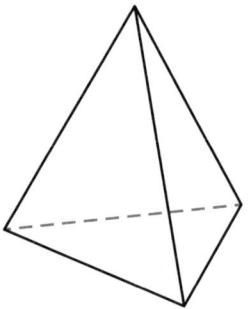

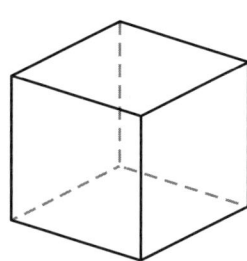

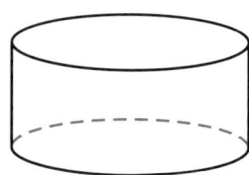

a. Eric wants to paint the solids. Colour the solids with the given descriptions.

green: solids with 5 vertices or more

red: solids with 6 edges

blue: solids with circular face(s)

b. If Eric has a rectangular pyramid in his collection, what colour should the solid be?

_____

c. Help Eric sort his solids.

• Solids that can roll:

_____

• Solids that can slide:

_____

• Solids that can be stacked:

_____

ISBN: 978-1-77149-201-0

⑤ Hugo has the nets below.

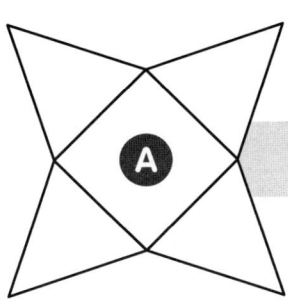 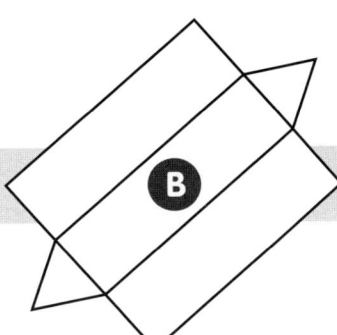 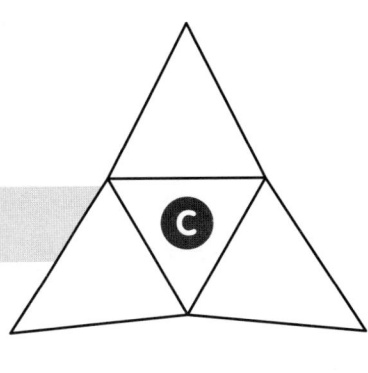

a. Which net folds into a triangular prism?

b. Which solid does Net A fold into?

_____

c. Does Net C fold into a solid that can be stacked?

d. Which net folds into a solid that has the fewest faces?

_____

e.

> This net folds into the same solid as Net A.

Is Hugo correct?

Hugo

_____

ISBN: 978-1-77149-201-0

⑥ Zara used her solids to make a picture.

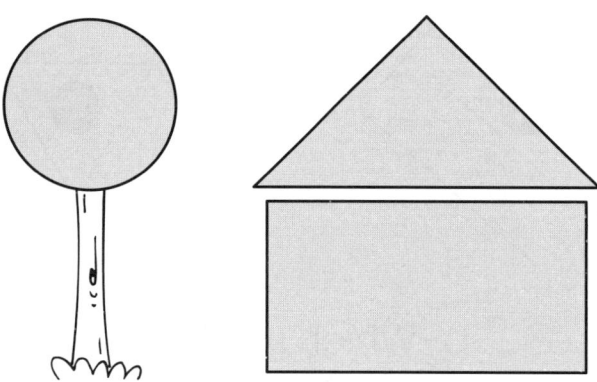

Zara's Solids

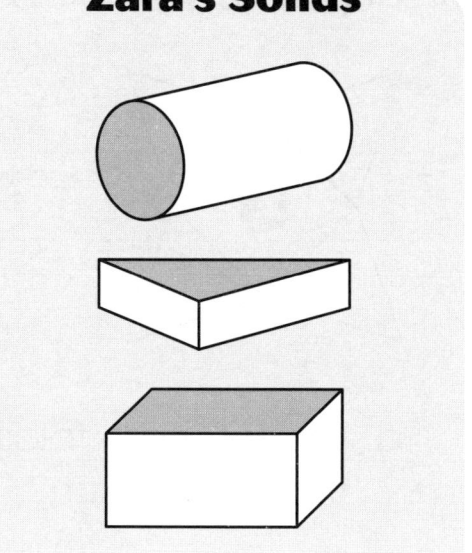

a. Which solid(s) did she use for

• the tree?

_____

• the house?

_____

b. Can a rectangular pyramid be used to make some of the prints in the picture? If so, name the prints it can make.

Hints

Do you know what the pyramids in Egypt look like?

_____

c. Zara wants to stack the solids to store them. Which ones can she stack?

_____

d. One of the solids rolled off her desk. Which one was it?

_____

ISBN: 978-1-77149-201-0

⑦ Jessie used all the sticks and marshmallows on the right to make a solid.

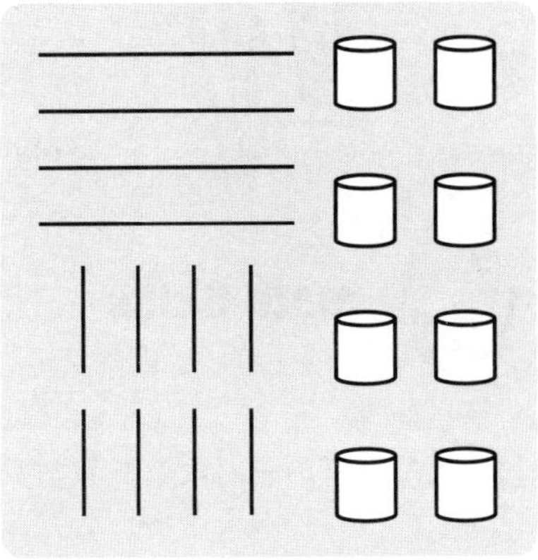

   a. What solid did she make?

   _____

   b. If Jessie used only 3 long sticks, 6 short sticks, and 6 marshmallows, what solid would she have made?

   _____

⑧ The children fold some nets.

   a. Mike's net has 6 squares. What solid does he make?

   _____

   b. Carley's net has 3 squares and 2 triangles. What solid does she make?

   _____

   c.

   My net has 2 fewer squares and 2 more triangles than Carley's. What solid is it?

   Jason

   _____

ISBN: 978-1-77149-201-0

Locations and Movements

solving a variety of word problems that involve grid maps and transformations

 **Math Skills**

① Sort the transformations. Write the letters.

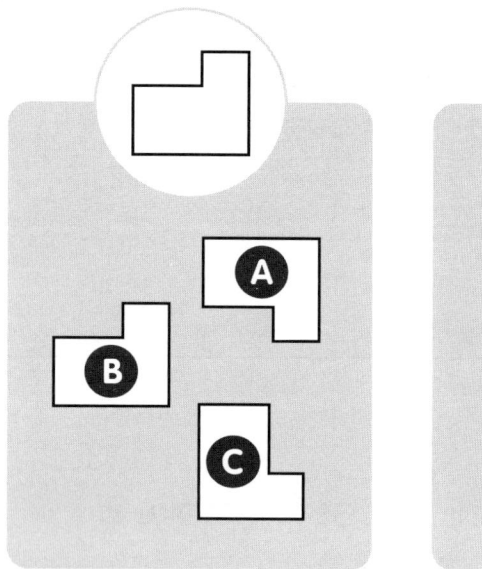

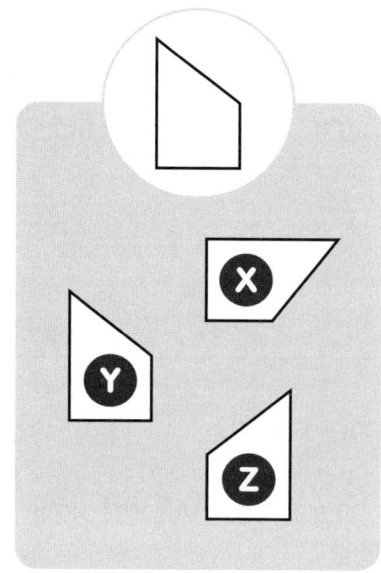

Translation:

_____

Rotation:

_____

Reflection:

_____

② This is a map of a flower garden.

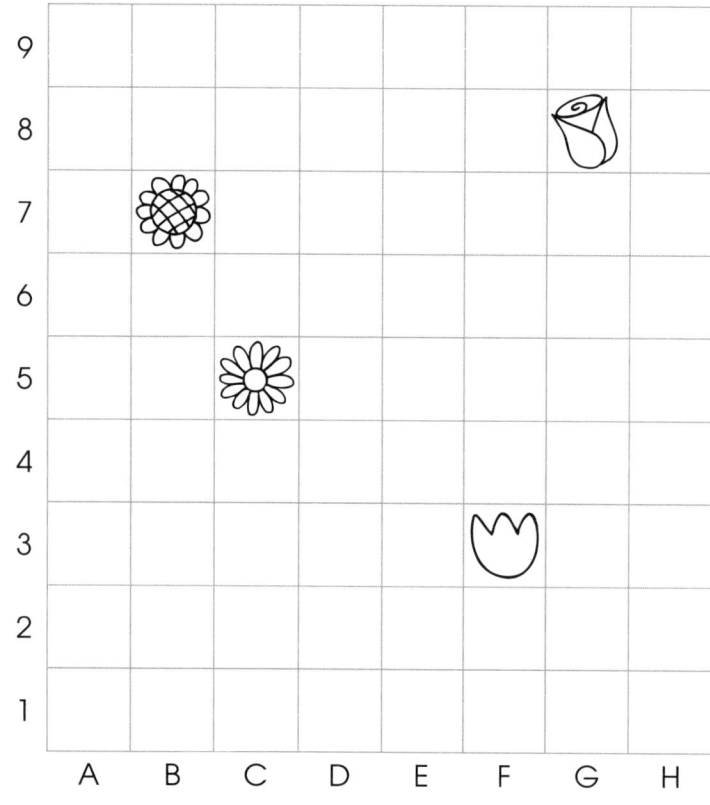

a. Locate the flowers.

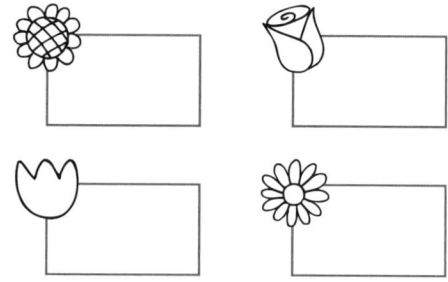

b. Draw a 🌸 at each of these locations.

A2	**E8**
D1	**H6**
G5	**C4**

ISBN: 978-1-77149-201-0

Problem Solving

Try This!

Carey the Cat wants to play with the fish. How should she go to reach the fish?

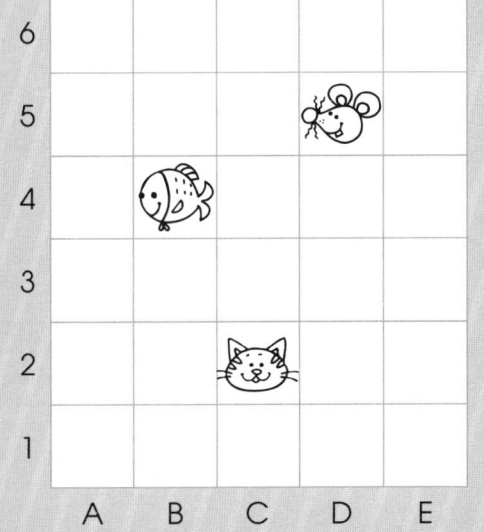

Solution:

Step 1: **Find Carey and the fish. Count the number of squares up from Carey.**

☐ square(s) up

Step 2: **Count the number of squares to the left.**

☐ square(s) to the left

Step 3: **Write a concluding sentence.**

Carey should go ☐ square(s) up and ☐ square(s) to the left.

① Refer to the map above.

a. Will Carey reach the fish if she goes 1 square to the left and 2 squares up?

_____ , Carey _____ reach the fish.
   Yes/No   will/will not

b. How should Carey go if she wants to play with the mouse instead?

Carey should go _____ and _____ .

ISBN: 978-1-77149-201-0

② A robber has just robbed a bank. A police officer is trying to catch him.

a. Locate the police officer and the robber.

b. There are road blocks 🚧 at D3 and E10. Draw them on the map.

c. If the police officer travels 2 squares up and 1 square to the left, will he catch the robber?

_____ , he _____
   Yes/No   will/will not

catch the robber.

d. The robber is now at A3.

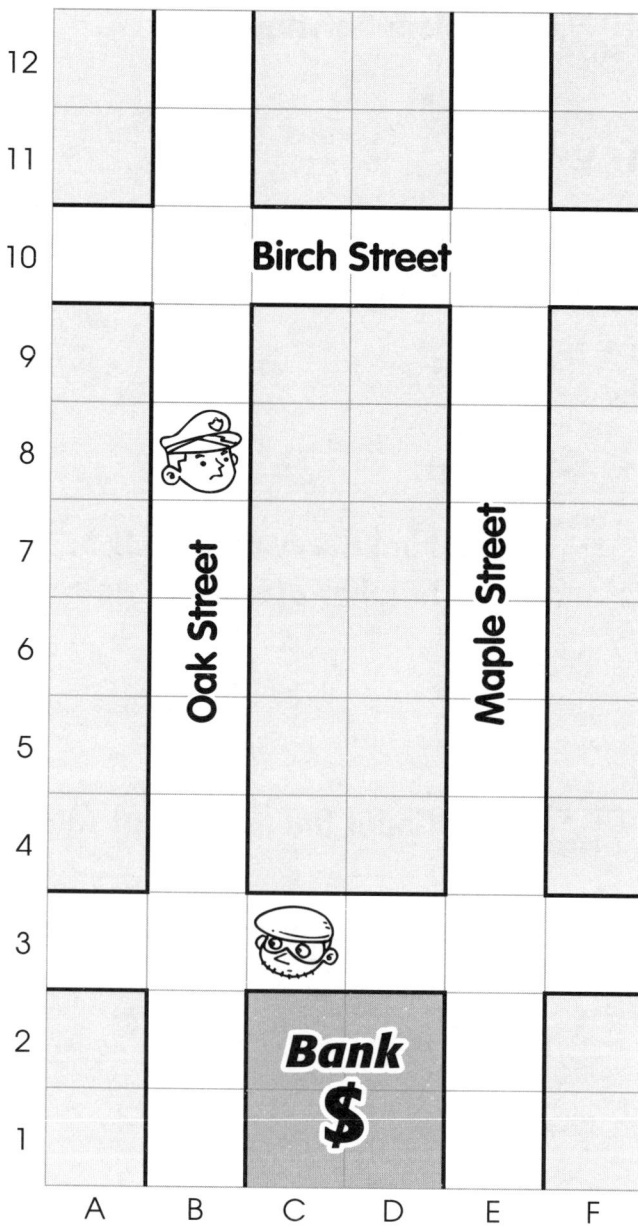

How should the police officer go to catch the robber?

The police officer should go _____

and _____ .

ISBN: 978-1-77149-201-0

③ Pirate Greg is looking for treasure.

Treasure Map

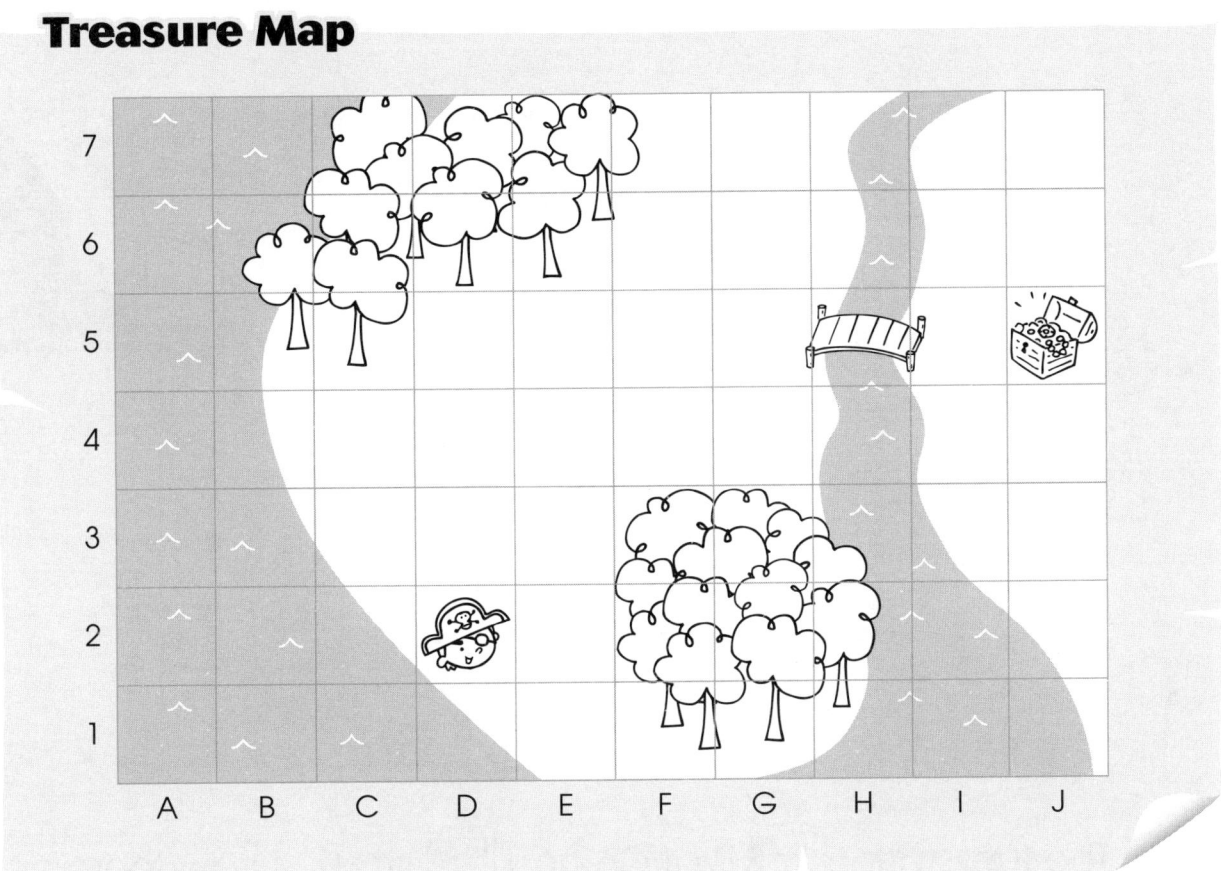

a. Locate the pirate and the treasure.

b. Draw a pirate ship and a big rock on the map.

c. How should Greg go to get the treasure?

Greg should go _____ and

_____ .

d.

How should I go to get back to my ship?

Greg should go _____

and _____ .

ISBN: 978-1-77149-201-0

④ A spaceship travelled to a space station. It avoided all the rocks.

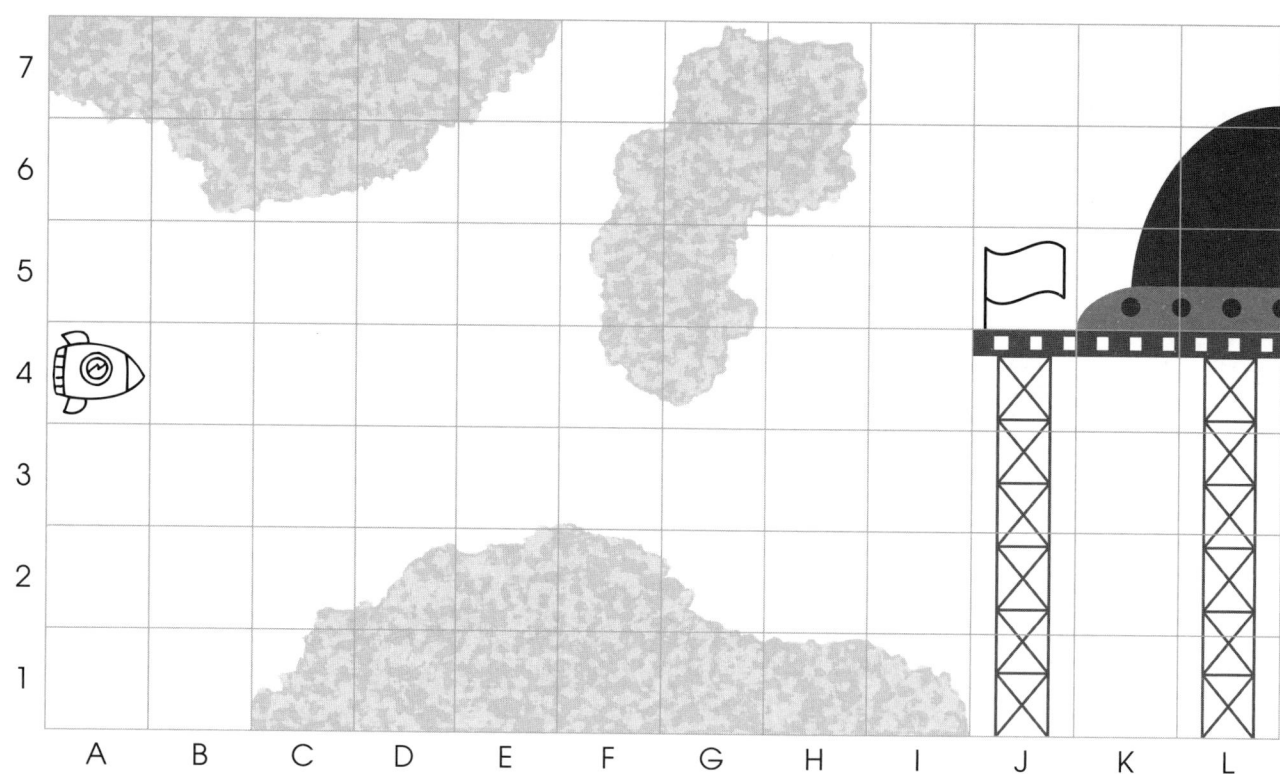

a. The fuel station 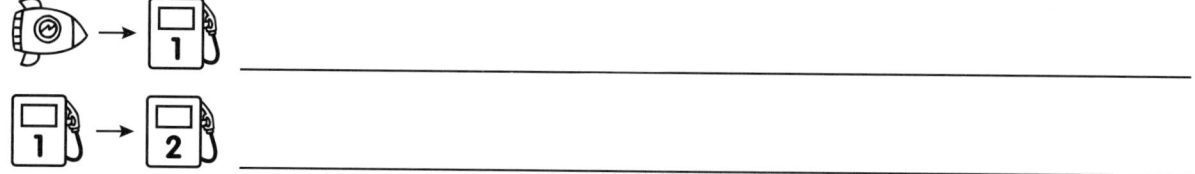 is at C6 and at H1. Draw them on the map.

b. The spaceship got fuel from both fuel stations. Describe its route to each fuel station.

c. After fuelling, the spaceship travelled 2 squares up and 1 square to the right and then broke down. Where did the spaceship break down? Draw a ✗ on the map

d. After repairs, the spaceship arrived at the space station at ⚐. How did the spaceship get there?

ISBN: 978-1-77149-201-0

⑤ Matt drew some shapes on a grid.

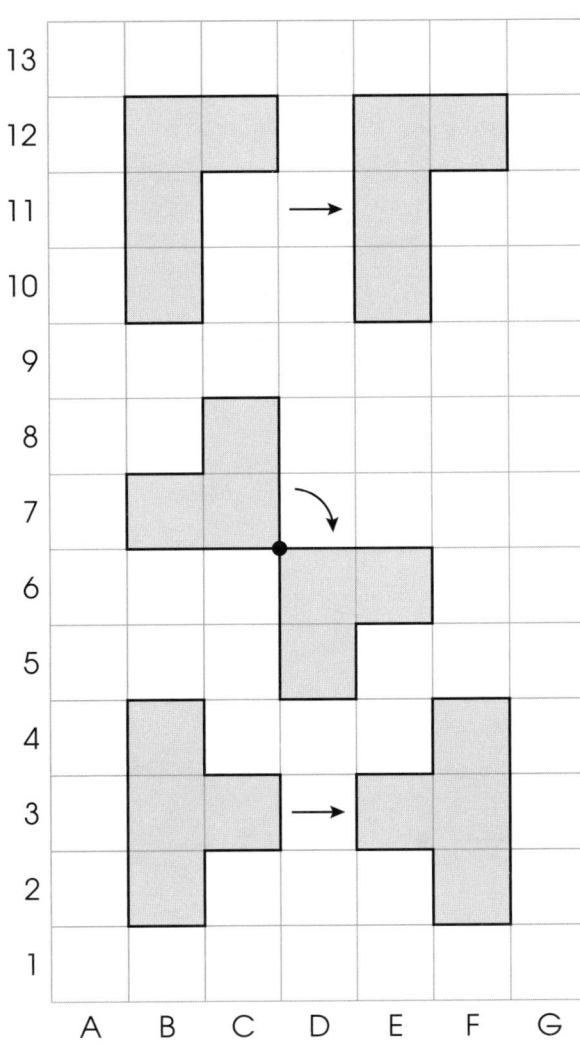

a. Name the transformation of each shape.

⌐ _____

⌐ _____

⌐ _____

b. Write the location of the squares that each original shape covers.

⌐ _____

⌐ _____

⌐ _____

c. Describe the transformation of ⌐ .

_____

d. If ⌐ is moved 3 squares down instead, on which square will it overlap another shape?

_____

Matt

ISBN: 978-1-77149-201-0

⑥

I'm taking some pictures at a petting zoo.

Elise's Camera

Elise

a. Name the squares to locate Elise's camera.

_____

b. Translate the camera 6 squares down and 1 square to the left. Which animal is Elise taking pictures of?

_____

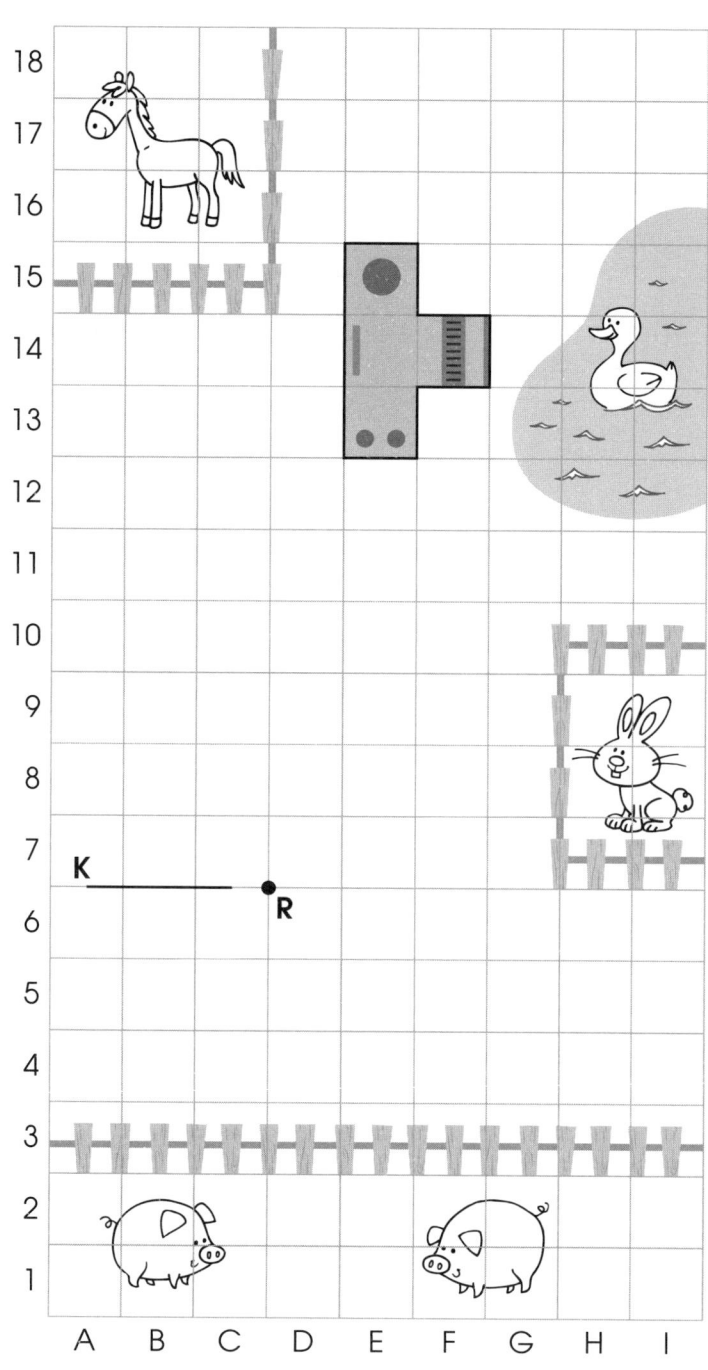

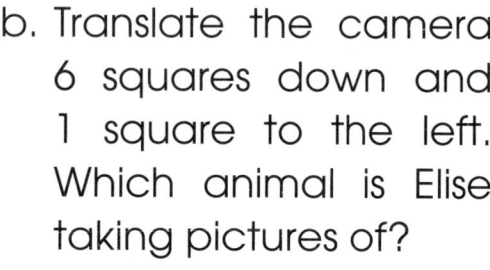

c. Rotate the camera $\frac{3}{4}$ clockwise about Point R. Which animal is Elise taking pictures of?

_____

d. Reflect the camera over Line K to take pictures of the pigs. Name the squares that the camera covers.

_____

ISBN: 978-1-77149-201-0

⑦ A building plan for a new library overlaps a pond.

The library must be at least 1 square space away from the pond, the railroad, and the streets.

a. The original plan for the library covers the squares below. Colour the area of the original library.

G6   H6   G5   H5   F4   G4   H4

b. A builder suggests moving the location of the library 3 squares up. Write the squares that the new location covers. Does this suggestion work? Explain.

c. Another builder suggests rotating the original location $\frac{1}{4}$ clockwise about Point R. Write the squares that the new location covers. Does this suggestion work? Explain.

ISBN: 978-1-77149-201-0

Data Management

solving a variety of word problems that involve pictographs, bar graphs, and circle graphs

Math Skills

① Complete the tables. Then match each data set with the correct pictograph.

A **Students' Lunches**

Food Item	Tally Marks	Number
pizza	IIII	
sandwich	II	
salad	III	

B **Students' Lunches**

Food Item	Tally Marks	Number
pizza	III	
sandwich	IIII	
salad	II	

C **Students' Lunches**

Food Item	Tally Marks	Number
pizza	HHH I	
sandwich	HHH III	
salad	IIII	

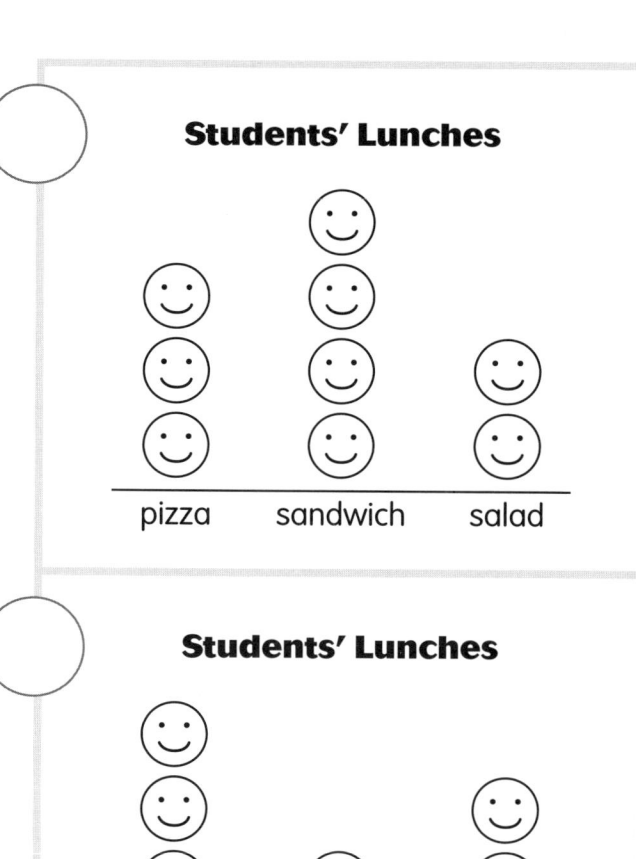

Students' Lunches

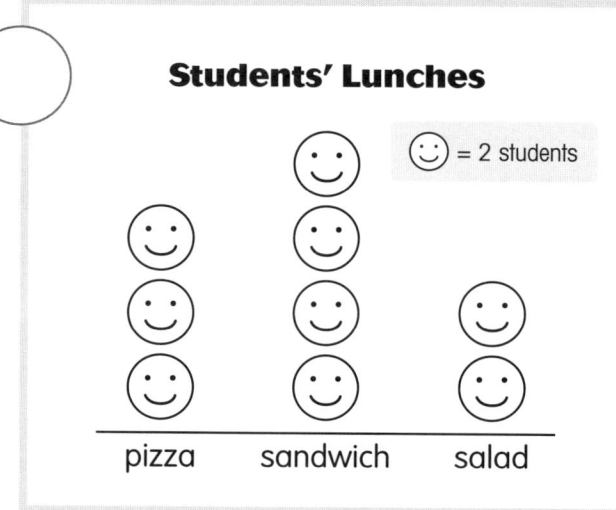

Students' Lunches

☺ = 2 students

ISBN: 978-1-77149-201-0

 **Problem Solving**

Jake and Joe both have pet fish. How many fish do they each have?

Number of Fish the Boys Have

= 2 fish

Jake   Joe

Solution:

Step 1: Check the legend.

= [ ] fish

Step 2: Read the pictograph.

Jake: 4 = [ ] fish

Joe: 3 = [ ] fish

Always check the legend before reading a graph.

Step 3: Write a concluding sentence.

Jake has [ ] fish and Joe has [ ] fish.

① Refer to the question above. If 1 🐟 represented 3 fish instead, how many fish would Jake and Joe have?

Jake would have _____ fish and Joe would have _____ fish.

ISBN: 978-1-77149-201-0

② Chef Carlos made a pictograph to show the meat his customers ordered at dinner.

Meat Ordered at Dinner

◎ = 2 customers

beef   pork   chicken   fish

a. Which meat was the most popular? Which one was the least popular?

_____ was the most popular and _____ was the least popular.

b. How many customers ordered pork?

Check the legend first.

_____ customers ordered pork.

c. How many customers ordered chicken?

_____ customers ordered chicken.

ISBN: 978-1-77149-201-0

d. How many more customers ordered pork than fish?

_____ more customer(s) ordered pork than fish.

e. How many customers ordered meat at dinner?

_____ customers ordered meat at dinner.

f.

> If 4 more customers ordered chicken, how many dishes would there be on the pictograph?

Chef Carlos

There would be _____ dishes.

③ A severe snowstorm caused a power outage at Sarah's and her friends' houses. Sarah recorded the number of hours that their houses had no power.

Number of Hours Without Power

Child	Linda	Ken	Sarah	Vason
Number of Hours	12	5	8	7

a. Complete the bar graph.

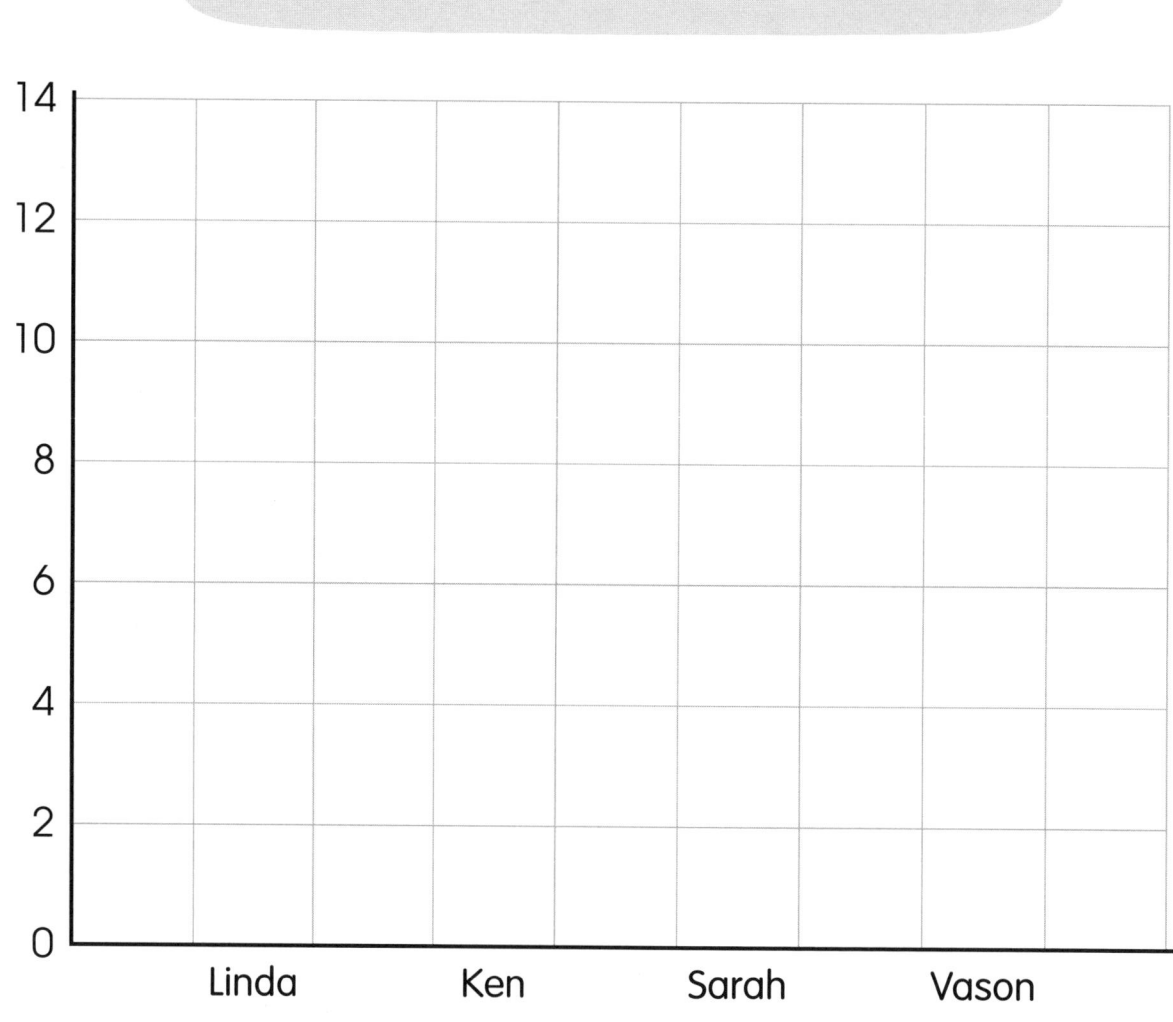

ISBN: 978-1-77149-201-0

b. Whose house went the longest time without power and for how many hours?

_____

c. How much longer did Linda's house remain without power than Ken's?

_____

d. Whose house went 1 hour more without power than Vason's?

_____

e.

If my house went 1 more hour without power, how many more blocks should I colour in the bar graph?

Sarah

_____

ISBN: 978-1-77149-201-0

④ Mrs. Lee's class voted for their favourite movie genres. The results are shown in the bar graph.

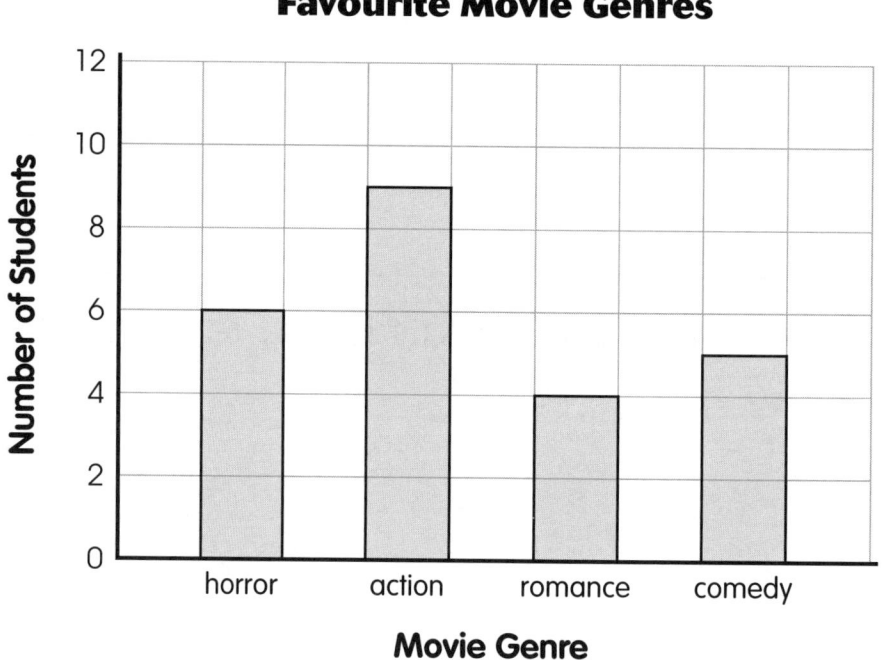

Favourite Movie Genres

a. Which movie genre is the most popular? How many students voted for that genre?

_____

b. Which movie genre is the least popular? How many students voted for that genre?

_____

c. How many more students voted for horror than romance?

_____

d. How many students are there in Mrs. Lee's class?

_____

ISBN: 978-1-77149-201-0

e. Which circle graph below shows the same data as the bar graph? Explain.

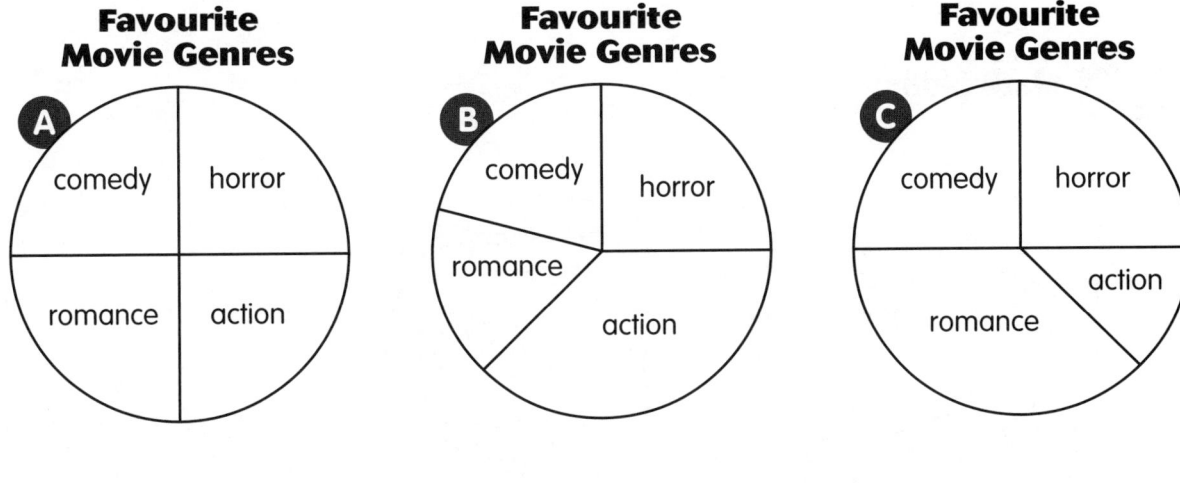

Favourite Movie Genres	**Favourite Movie Genres**	**Favourite Movie Genres**

_____

_____

f. Which graph should be used to show that $\frac{1}{4}$ of the class voted for horror, the bar graph or the circle graph?

_____

g. Which graph should be used to show that 9 students voted for action, the bar graph or the circle graph?

_____

h. Would a bar graph be a better choice to show that more students voted for action than comedy?

_____

i. Mrs. Lee is deciding on a movie for a class outing. Should she pick an action movie or a romance movie?

_____

ISBN: 978-1-77149-201-0

Probability

solving a variety of word problems that involve determining the probability of outcomes

 **Math Skills**

①

impossible / likely

②

certain / unlikely

③

likely / impossible

④

unlikely / certain

⑤

I will flip heads or tails.

unlikely / equally likely

⑥

unlikely / certain

⑦ an airplane flying under water

likely / impossible

⑧ going to bed in the morning

impossible / unlikely

⑨ building a snowman in the summer

impossible / unlikely

⑩ a baby being a boy or a girl

unlikely / equally likely

⑪ a flower blooming in spring

likely / unlikely

ISBN: 978-1-77149-201-0

 **Problem Solving**

Try This!

I am picking a ball from this box. What is the chance of picking an odd number?

Amelia

Solution:

Step 1: Count the number of balls.

[ ] balls in total

[ ] balls with an odd number (① and ③)

└ More than half of the balls have an odd number.

Step 2: Write a concluding sentence.

The chance of picking an odd number is [ ] .

① Refer to the question above.

a. What is the chance of picking a ball that has an even number?

b. What is the chance of picking a ball that has a number greater than 3?

The chance of picking a ball that has an even number is _____ .

The chance of picking a ball that has a number greater than 3 is _____ .

② This dice is labelled 1 to 6 on its 6 sides. I will roll this dice once.

a. Are all the numbers equally likely to be rolled?

_____ , they _____ equally likely
Yes/No   are/are not

to be rolled.

b. What is the chance of rolling

• a "4"?

• a number that is greater than "0"?

It is _____ .

It is _____ .

• a "3" or a "6"?

• a number that is less than "0"?

It is _____ .

It is _____ .

• a "7"?

• a number that is between "2" and "4"?

It is _____ .

It is _____ .

ISBN: 978-1-77149-201-0

③ Luna picks one card from below.

| A | 2 | 3 | 1 | K | 2 | 6 | 4 | E |

a. What is the chance of picking

- a letter?

- a number?

It is _____ .

It is _____ .

- an even number?

- a vowel?  **Hints**

The vowels are
a, e, i, o, and u.

It is _____ .

It is _____ .

b. Is Luna more likely to pick a vowel or an even number?

Luna is more likely to pick a(n) _____ .

c.

Luna

I removed one card so that there are 8 cards in total, and the chance of picking an "A" or a "2" is equally likely.

Which card was removed?

A " _____ " card was removed.

ISBN: 978-1-77149-201-0

④ At a game booth, Kayla spins one of the wheels below. She will win the toy animal that the pointer lands on.

Spinner A

a. On Spinner A, what is the chance of getting

• a toy dog?

_____

• a toy cat?

_____

Spinner B

b. On Spinner B, what is the chance of getting

• a toy bear?

_____

• a toy snake?

_____

c. Which spinner is Kayla describing?

• "It is equally likely to get a toy bear or a toy dog."

_____

• "It is impossible to get a toy pig."

_____

d. If Kayla wants to win a toy cat, does it matter which spinner she spins? If so, which one should she spin?

_____

ISBN: 978-1-77149-201-0

⑤ Look at Jennifer's and Alex's boxes. Colour the balls using the given descriptions.

Jennifer's Box

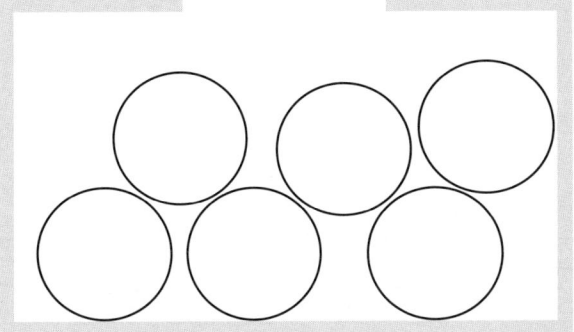

Alex's Box

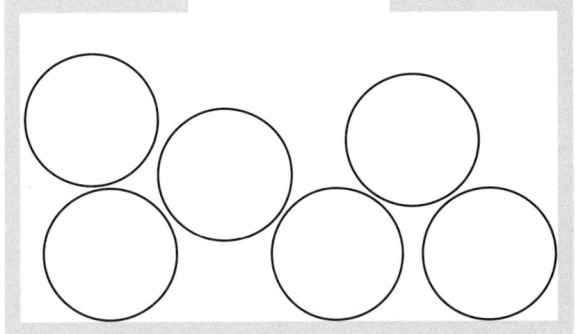

a. • It is equally likely to pick a red ball or a yellow ball.

• It is unlikely to pick a blue ball.

• It is less likely to pick a green ball than a yellow ball.

b. What is the chance of picking a yellow ball?

_____

c. What is the chance of picking a pink ball?

_____

d. • It is likely to pick a blue ball.

• It is equally likely to pick a red ball or a yellow ball.

• It is impossible to pick a green ball.

e. What is the chance of picking a red ball?

_____

f. What is the chance of picking a ball that is not blue?

_____

g.  I want to pick a yellow ball. Whose box should I pick from?

Jim

_____

ISBN: 978-1-77149-201-0

⑥ Jack wants to make a card game with a deck of 6 cards using the letters **X**, **Y**, and **Z**.

a. If he wants the chance of drawing an **X** to be certain, what should he do?

_____

b. If he wants the chance of drawing an **X**, a **Y**, or a **Z** to be the same, what should he do?

_____

c. If he wants the chance of drawing a **Y** to be impossible, what should he do?

_____

d. If he wants the chance of drawing a **Y** or a **Z** to be equally likely, what should he do?

💡**Hints**

There is more than one answer.

e.

I drew a card 20 times from the deck. The number of times that each letter was drawn is recorded here.

Jack

How many **Z** cards could there be in the deck?

Results

5 X 5 Y 10 Z

_____

ISBN: 978-1-77149-201-0

⑦ Lucy is at a game booth that has 3 games. The results of 30 trials of each game are recorded in the table.

Results of 30 Trials of Each Game

Game \ No. of Times	✏️	🚗	🍬
Pick a Ball!	0	15	15
Draw a Card!	10	11	9
Spin It!	26	2	2

a. How likely is it for Lucy to win a candy from "Draw a Card!"?

_____

b. How likely is it for Lucy to win a crayon from "Spin It!"?

_____

c. If Lucy wants a toy car or a candy, which game should she play?

_____

d. If Lucy does not want a crayon, which game should she play?

_____

e. Lucy thinks that it is likely that there are no balls with crayons in "Pick a Ball!". Is she correct? Explain.

_____

ISBN: 978-1-77149-201-0

ISBN: 978-1-77149-201-0

Section 2:
Critical-thinking Questions

ISBN: 978-1-77149-201-0

Students are required to solve multi-step questions which involve various topics in each.

Topics Covered

	Number Sense and Numeration	Measurement	Geometry and Spatial Sense	Patterning and Algebra	Data Management and Probability	My Record ✔ correct ✗ incorrect
1	multiplication subtraction					☐
2	division	perimeter				☐
3	multiplication	temperature				☐
4	money			patterning		☐
5		capacity			data management	☐
6		perimeter	locations movements			☐
7			solids		probability	☐
8	multiplication division					☐
9	fractions	mass				☐
10	addition				data management	☐
11	fractions	time		patterning		☐
12	money				probability	☐
13	multiplication division					☐
14	addition division					☐
15		perimeter area	locations			☐
16			shapes	patterning		☐
17	division	perimeter	shapes			☐
18	fractions decimals					☐
19	fractions decimals					☐
20	money	time				☐

ISBN: 978-1-77149-201-0

① One pack of chocolate squares has 3 rows and 3 columns. Kirk's family finishes 8 packs. If Kirk's family had 180 chocolate squares, how many chocolate squares remain?

No. of chocolate squares in 1 pack: _____ × _____ = _____

No. of chocolate squares in 8 packs: _____ × _____ = _____

Remaining no. of chocolate squares: _____ – _____ = _____

_____ chocolate squares remain.

② The perimeter of Square A is 16 cm. The perimeter of Square B is half of Square A's. How much longer is the side length of Square A than Square B?

Hints

Remember, all sides of a square are the same length.

③ July's highest temperature was 9 times March's and its lowest temperature was 23°C warmer than March's. If the highest temperature in March was 4°C and the lowest temperature was 0°C, what were the highest and lowest temperatures in July?

④ Eunice spent $3.50 on stationery in January, $4 in February, and $4.50 in March. If the pattern continues, how much will she spend in May?

Topics covered:

Question 1	**Question 2**	**Question 3**	**Question 4**
• multiplication	• division	• multiplication	• money
• subtraction	• perimeter	• temperature	• patterning

ISBN: 978-1-77149-201-0

⑤ The bar graph shows the capacities of cup sizes. If Emily orders 2 small, 1 medium, and 1 large cups of juice, how many millilitres of juice does she have in total?

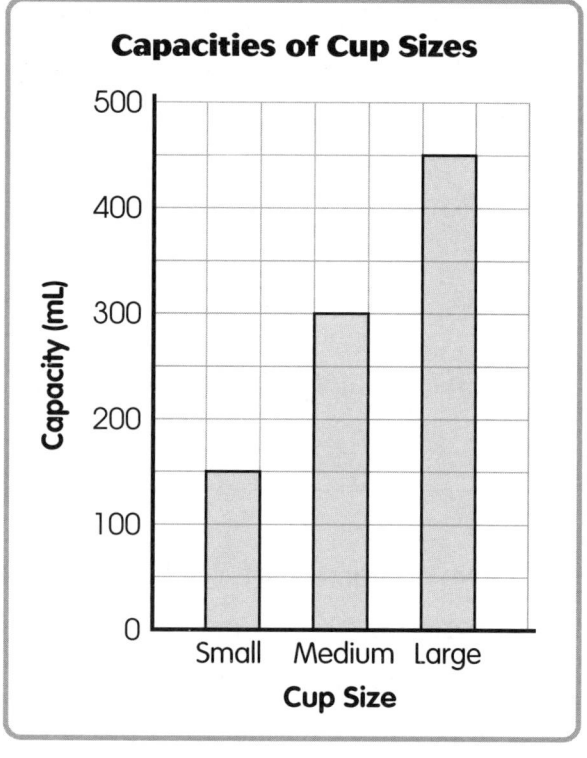

⑥ The figure is translated 3 squares down and 1 square to the right. Draw the translated figure and write the squares that it covers. What is its perimeter?

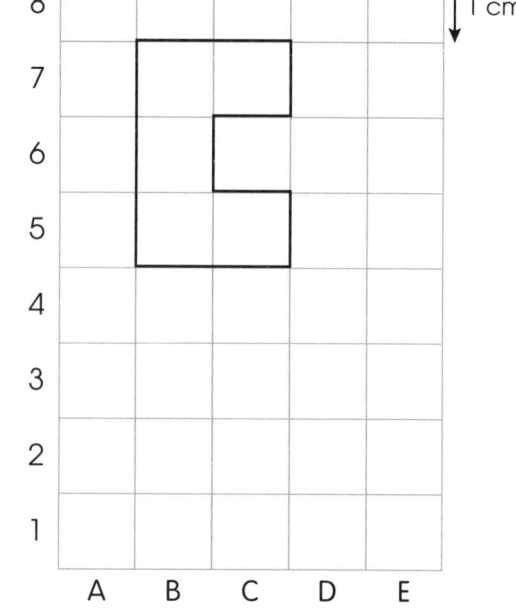

Topics covered:

Question 5
- capacity
- data management

Question 6
- perimeter
- locations
- movements

ISBN: 978-1-77149-201-0

⑦ Nancy picks one of the solids randomly. What is her chance of picking a solid with 6 faces?

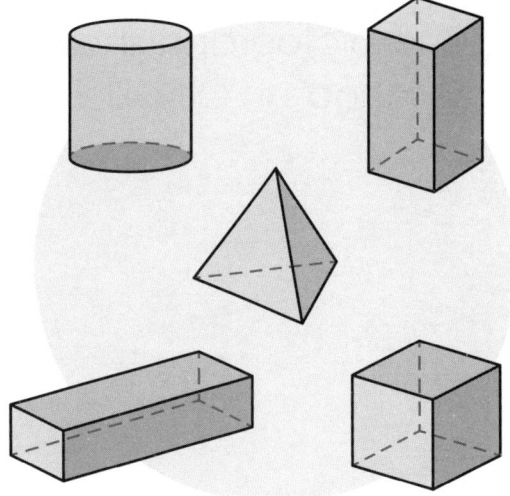

⑧ One package has 16 socks. How many pairs of socks are there in 5 packages?

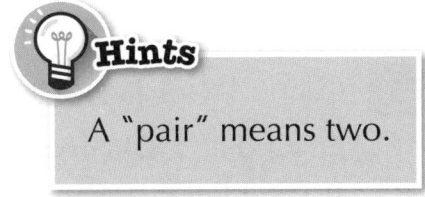

A "pair" means two.

⑨ Mike has books and toys in a box and they weigh 10 kg in all. Each book weighs 2 kg and each toy weighs 1 kg. If there are 2 books in the box, what fraction of the total mass are the toys? Find the mass of the toys in grams.

Topics covered:

Question 7	**Question 8**	**Question 9**
• solids	• multiplication	• fractions
• probability	• division	• mass

ISBN: 978-1-77149-201-0

The pictograph shows the number of students at each of the 3 schools in Cityville. How many students are there in Cityville?

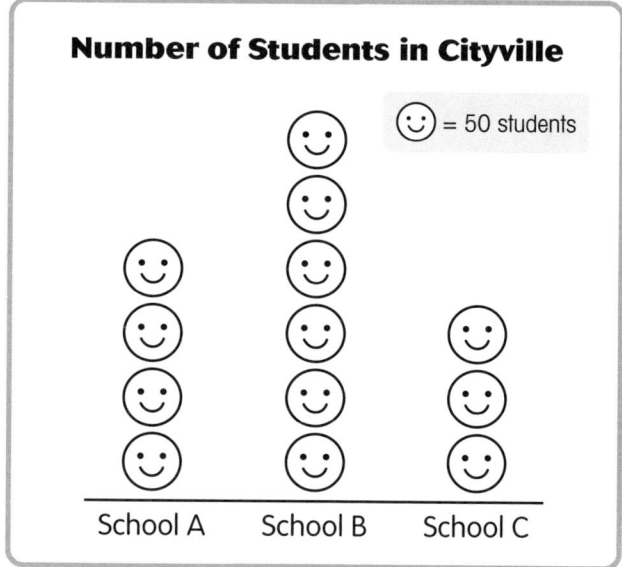

Number of Students in Cityville

☺ = 50 students

School A   School B   School C

⑪ Chris had half an hour of soccer drills on August 7, 13, 19, 25, and 31. How frequently did Chris have soccer drills? How much time did he spend on soccer drills in August?

		August 2015				
Sun	Mon	Tue	Wed	Thu	Fri	Sat
						1
2	3	4	5	6	7	8
9	10	11	12	13	14	15
16	17	18	19	20	21	22
23	24	25	26	27	28	29
30	31					

Topics covered:

Question 10
• addition
• data management

Question 11
• fractions
• time
• patterning

ISBN: 978-1-77149-201-0

⑫ The coins in Melissa's jar are shown. If she uses one of the coins, what is the chance that exactly $0.50 will be left in her jar?

⑬ Rick's toy cars were put into 6 rows of 4 columns. He rearranged them into 8 rows. How many columns of cars does he have?

⑭ To assemble a stool, 4 legs are needed. Mr. Frank has assembled 234 stools and has 40 stool legs left to assemble. How many stools will Mr. Frank have in all?

Topics covered:

Question 12	Question 13	Question 14
• money	• multiplication	• addition
• probability	• division	• division

ISBN: 978-1-77149-201-0

Yvonne's rectangular tomato garden covers 12 squares on the grid. C2, C4, F2, and F4 are the four corners of the garden. Yvonne wants to put a fence around the garden. How many metres of fencing does she need?

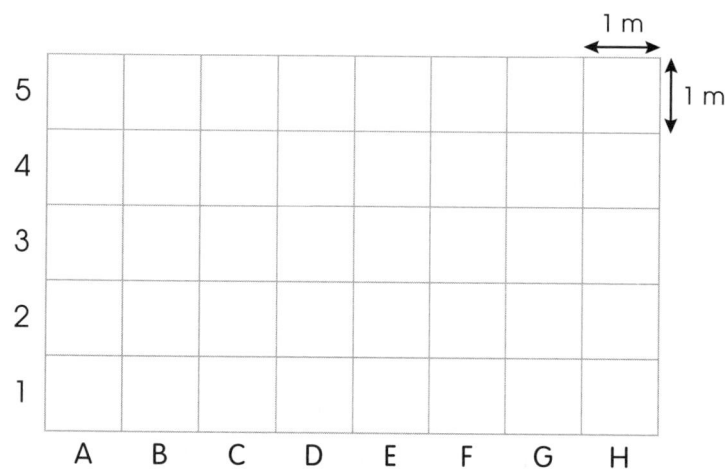

⑯ Identify two attributes that both of these patterns share. Describe the attributes.

Pattern A:

Pattern B:

Topics covered:

Question 15
- perimeter
- area
- locations

Question 16
- shapes
- patterning

ISBN: 978-1-77149-201-0

⑰ The perimeter of a regular hexagon measures 42 cm. What is the length of one side of the hexagon?

Tips

All sides of a regular hexagon are equal in length.

⑱ Joe's pizzas were each divided into 10 slices. 0.1 of the cheese pizza is left and 0.2 of the Canadian pizza is left. What fraction of the pizzas were eaten? Write your answer as a mixed fraction.

⑲ Wanda bought $\frac{1}{2}$ of 6 oranges, $\frac{3}{4}$ of 8 apples, and 0.2 of 10 pears. How many fruits did Wanda buy in all?

⑳ Mr. Jake earns $25.50 every hour. If Mr. Jake works from start to finish as shown on the clocks, how much does he earn?

Start

Finish

Topics covered:

Question 17	Question 18	Question 19	Question 20
• division	• fractions	• fractions	• money
• perimeter	• decimals	• decimals	• time
• shapes			

ISBN: 978-1-77149-201-0

Students are required to solve multi-step questions which involve various topics in each.

Topics Covered

	Number Sense and Numeration	Measurement	Geometry and Spatial Sense	Patterning and Algebra	Data Management and Probability	My Record ✔ correct ✘ incorrect
1	multiplication division					
2	money			patterning		
3		time temperature		patterning		
4	addition	mass				
5		time			data management	
6		area	locations movements			
7	multiplication	capacity				
8	fractions		shapes			
9	addition	perimeter				
10	division money					
11	decimals				probability	
12	fractions	time				
13	division		solids			
14	multiplication money					
15	fractions	area				
16		area	shapes			
17				patterning	data management	
18	decimals money					
19	subtraction				probability	
20			locations movements	patterning		

ISBN: 978-1-77149-201-0

① One paper flower has 5 petals. Each bouquet of flowers has 30 petals. How many flowers are there in 2 bouquets?

No. of flowers in 1 bouquet: _____ ÷ _____ = _____

No. of flowers in 2 bouquets: _____ × _____ = _____

There are _____ in 2 bouquets.

② Monica saved $1.25 on Monday, $1.50 on Tuesday, and $1.75 on Wednesday. If the pattern continues, how much will she save on Friday?

③ Each hour, the temperature rises by 2°C. If it is 3°C at 9:00 a.m., what will the temperature be by noon?

Tips

"Noon" means 12:00 p.m.

④ A big block is 3 kg and a small block is 2 kg. Bethany places 2 big blocks on one side of the scale. How many small blocks should she place on the other side to balance the scale?

**Hints**

You can draw a scale to illustrate your thinking.

Topics covered:

Question 1	**Question 2**	**Question 3**	**Question 4**
• multiplication	• money	• time	• addition
• division	• patterning	• temperature	• mass
		• patterning	

⑤ The bar graph shows the amount of time Devon spent on reading in a day. How many hours did he spend on reading in total?

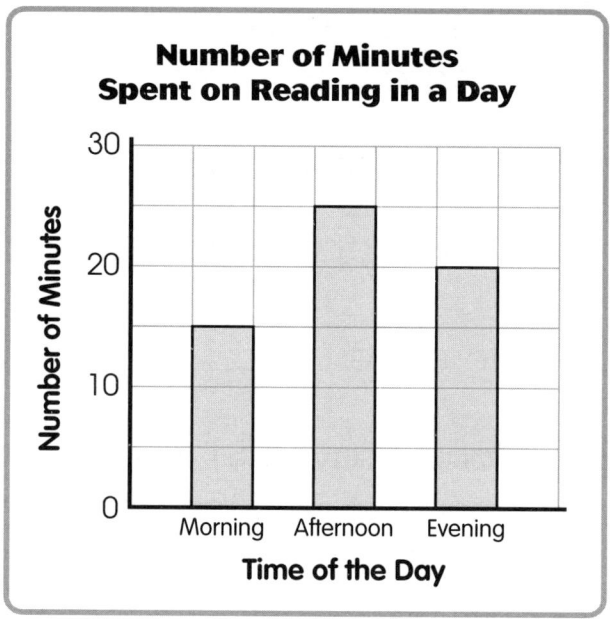

⑥ Kelly reflects the shaded part over Line K to complete a shape. Name the squares that the shape covers completely. What is the area of the shape?

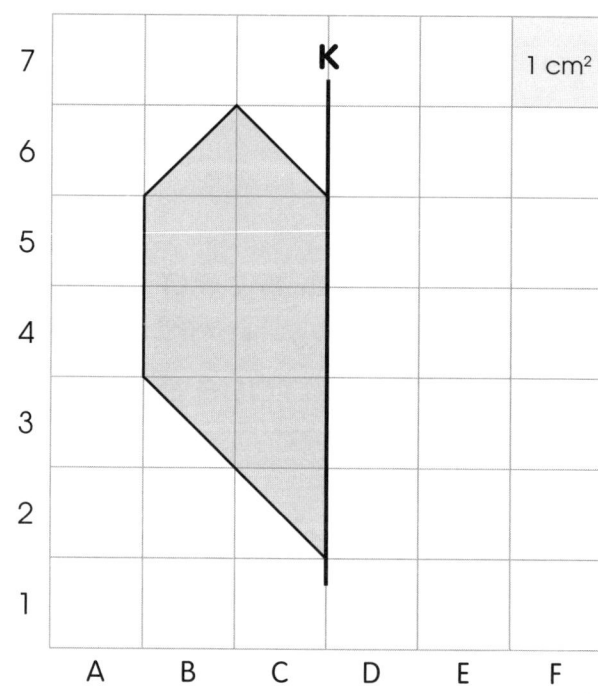

Topics covered:

Question 5
- time
- data management

Question 6
- area
- locations
- movements

ISBN: 978-1-77149-201-0

⑦ Milk is sold in cartons of 2 L. Thomas buys 4 cartons of milk. How much milk does he have in millilitres?

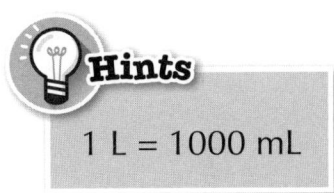

Hints

1 L = 1000 mL

⑧ Harry cut out 2 parallelograms, 3 rhombuses, 2 squares, 2 kites, and 1 rectangle. What fraction of the shapes that Harry cut out have 2 or more lines of symmetry?

⑨ Jordan has a 190 cm by 160 cm garden in his backyard. The garden is 2 m away from the edge of his backyard on all sides. What is the perimeter of Jordan's backyard in centimetres?

Hints

1 m = 100 cm

Topics covered:

Question 7	**Question 8**	**Question 9**
• multiplication	• shapes	• addition
• capacity	• fractions	• perimeter

ISBN: 978-1-77149-201-0

10 Heather had saved up for 5 days for her mother's gift. She paid for a $12.45 gift with all her savings and got $2.55 back in change. How much did she save each day?

11 Mindy has a jar of 20 marbles. 0.5 of them are purple, 0.3 are pink, and the rest are red. What is the probability of picking a marble that is not red or purple?

12 Caleb spends 45 minutes on homework each day. How many hours does he spend doing homework in 3 days? Write your answer as a mixed fraction.

Topics covered:

Question 10	Question 11	Question 12
• division	• decimals	• fractions
• money	• probability	• time

ISBN: 978-1-77149-201-0

⑬ The edges of a square-based pyramid are the same length. The total length of all the edges is 56 cm. What is the length of one edge?

⑭ A pie store sells slices of pie for $3 each and gives a $1.25 discount for every 3 slices of pie bought. If Jill bought 9 slices of pie, how much did she pay?

⑮ A floor is covered by 20 slabs. Each slab is 1 m². $\frac{1}{4}$ of the slabs are white and the rest are black. How much greater is the area that the black slabs cover than the white slabs?

Topics covered:

Question 13	**Question 14**	**Question 15**
• division	• multiplication	• fractions
• solids	• money	• area

⑯ Kyle made the kite below using 2 identical triangles. Draw a line to divide the kite into the 2 triangles. What is the area of each triangle?

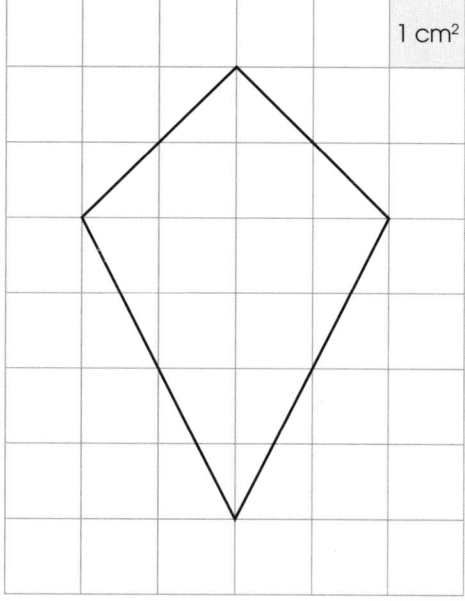

1 cm²

⑰ The number of flowers that bloomed each week is shown. If the pattern continues, how many flowers will bloom in Week 6?

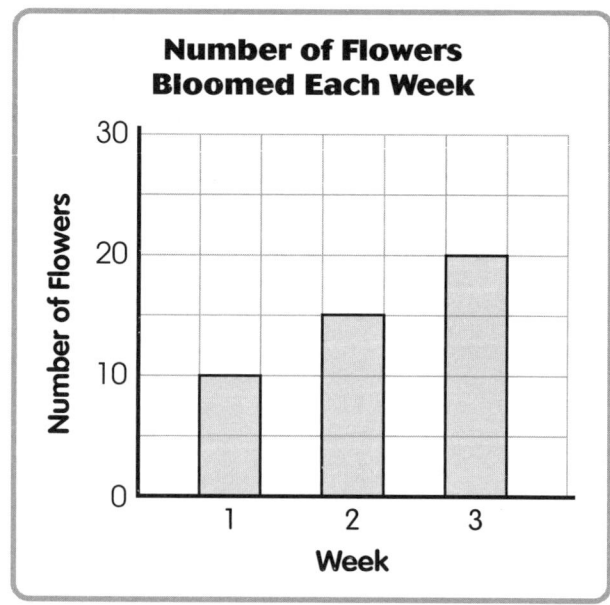

Topics covered:

Question 16
- area
- shapes

Question 17
- patterning
- data management

ISBN: 978-1-77149-201-0

⑱ Jack has 10 coins. If 0.2 of them are toonies, 0.7 of them are quarters, and the rest are loonies, how much money does Jack have?

⑲ Hector's jar contains 800 jelly beans. 127 are red, 473 are green, and the rest are blue. How likely is it for Hector to pick a jelly bean that is not blue?

⑳ Amy follows a pattern to draw smiley faces on the grid. What is the pattern rule? Draw the next smiley face.

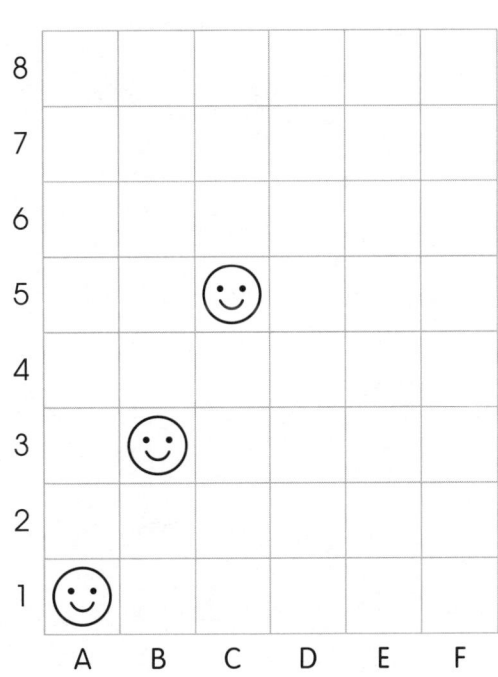

Topics covered:

Question 18
- decimals
- money

Question 19
- subtraction
- probability

Question 20
- locations
- movements
- patterning

ISBN: 978-1-77149-201-0

Students are required to solve multi-step questions which involve various topics in each.

Topics Covered

	Number Sense and Numeration	Measurement	Geometry and Spatial Sense	Patterning and Algebra	Data Management and Probability	My Record ✔ correct ✘ incorrect
1	multiplication division					
2		perimeter	solids			
3	division	mass				
4	subtraction multiplication					
5	multiplication money	time				
6	fractions				data management	
7	fractions	temperature				
8	multiplication division	perimeter				
9	fractions decimals	perimeter				
10	money		shapes			
11	decimals	capacity				
12	money			patterning		
13		time		patterning		
14		area	locations movements			
15				patterning	data management	
16	division		solids			
17	division money					
18			shapes		probability	
19					probability / data management	
20	addition	time			data management	

ISBN: 978-1-77149-201-0

① There are 5 mangoes in a box. It takes 3 mangoes to make a tray of mango pudding. If there are 6 boxes, how many trays of mango pudding can be made?

Total number of mangoes: _____ × _____ = _____

Number of trays: _____ ÷ _____ = _____

_____ of mango pudding can be made.

② A cube's edge is 6 cm long. What is the perimeter of 1 of its faces?

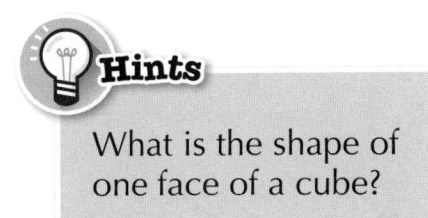

What is the shape of one face of a cube?

③ Teresa harvested some melons that weighed a total of 48 kg. If each melon weighed 8000 g, how many melons did Teresa harvest?

④ A pet store has 225 pets. There are 9 fish in each of the 7 tanks. How many pets in the pet store are not fish?

Topics covered:

Question 1	Question 2	Question 3	Question 4
• multiplication	• perimeter	• division	• subtraction
• division	• solids	• mass	• multiplication

ISBN: 978-1-77149-201-0

⑤ In June, Billy spent $8 on a swimming lesson every Thursday. He also spent $8.75 for a school trip and $6.50 for a new notebook. How much money did Billy spend in all?

June 2016						
Sun	Mon	Tue	Wed	Thu	Fri	Sat
			1	2	3	4
5	6	7	8	9	10	11
12	13	14	15	16	17	18
19	20	21	22	23	24	25
26	27	28	29	30		

⑥ A pictograph shows the favourite pizza toppings of the students. The number of students who voted ham was $\frac{1}{3}$ of those who voted cheese. Complete the pictograph. How many students voted in all?

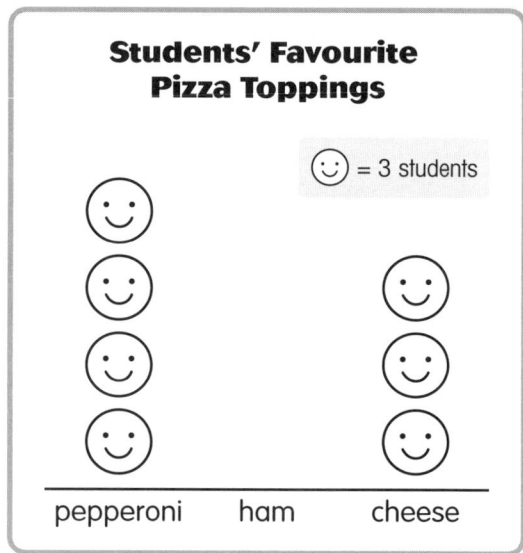

Topics covered:

Question 5
- multiplication
- money
- time

Question 6
- fractions
- data management

ISBN: 978-1-77149-201-0

⑦ It was 2°C in the morning and twice as warm in the afternoon. In the evening, the temperature was $\frac{1}{4}$ of that in the afternoon. What were the temperatures in the afternoon and evening?

⑧ Clement plants 2 seeds for every 8 cm around a rectangular frame. The frame measures 30 cm by 10 cm. How many seeds will Clement plant?

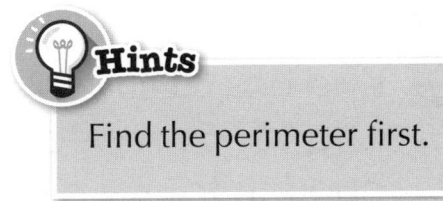

Hints

Find the perimeter first.

⑨ Ray's backyard is 20 m in length and 10 m in width. The length of Ann's backyard is $\frac{1}{4}$ the length of Ray's and 0.5 the width of Ray's. What is the perimeter of Ann's backyard?

Topics covered:

Question 7	**Question 8**	**Question 9**
• fractions	• multiplication	• fractions
• temperature	• division	• decimals
	• perimeter	• perimeter

ISBN: 978-1-77149-201-0

⑩ Carlos wants to build a triangular frame that measures 1 m on each side. A 1-m long plank costs $12.95. How much money does Carlos need to spend on the planks?

⑪ For 20 L of fruit punch, 0.3 of it is orange juice, 0.4 is apple juice, 0.1 is lemon juice, and the rest is lime juice. How many millilitres of lime juice is there?

⑫ Kyle has $3.45 in his piggy bank on Monday, $6.20 on Tuesday, and $8.95 on Wednesday. If the pattern continues, will he have enough to buy a soccer ball that costs $14.25 by Friday?

⑬ Stacey took breaks from work at 12:45, 1:20, and 1:55. How many more breaks will Stacey take by 3:00? What times will she take those breaks?

Topics covered:

Question 10	**Question 11**	**Question 12**	**Question 13**
• money	• decimals	• money	• time
• shapes	• capacity	• patterning	• patterning

ISBN: 978-1-77149-201-0

⑭ A stone path is paved from D1 to D7. Another flower garden that is a reflection of the existing one over the stone path is also added. What is the total area of the flower gardens?

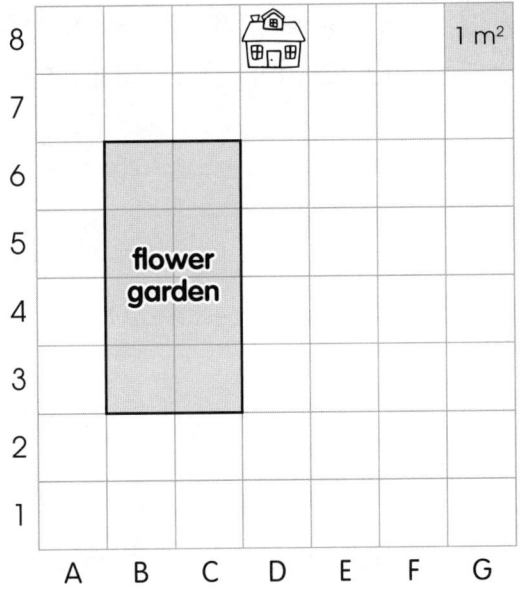

⑮ The bar graph shows the number of students attending Meadow Ridge Public School each year. If the pattern continues, how many students will there be in 2018?

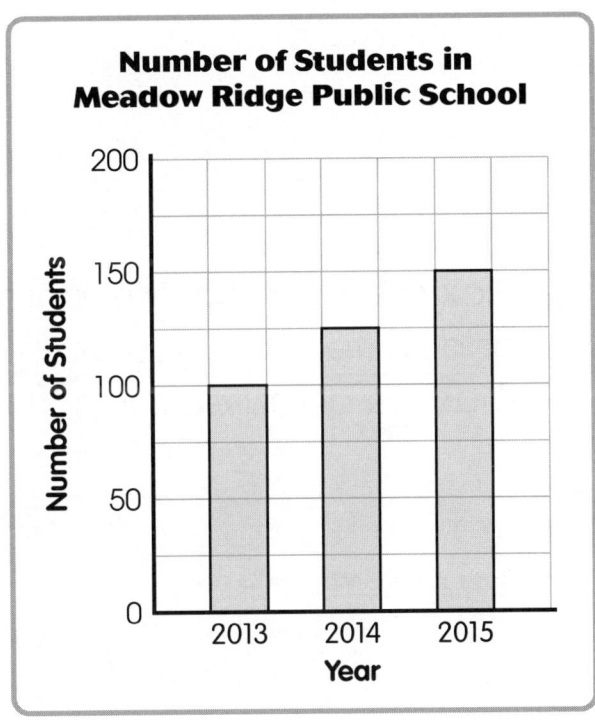

Topics covered:

Question 14
- area
- locations
- movements

Question 15
- patterning
- data management

ISBN: 978-1-77149-201-0

⑯ The area of a cube's net is 24 cm². What is the total area of 2 faces on the cube?

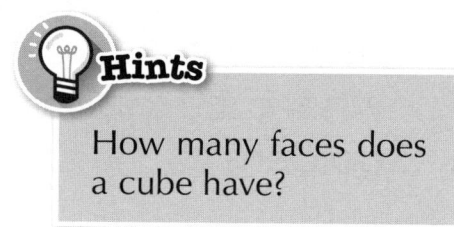

Hints

How many faces does a cube have?

⑰ A $20 dinner bill was split equally among 4 people. Michael paid with a $10 bill. What was his change in the fewest coins?

⑱ Rick drew a rhombus, a trapezoid, a parallelogram, a triangle, and a kite. He coloured one of the shapes. What is the chance that the coloured shape has more than 1 line of symmetry?

Topics covered:

Question 16	**Question 17**	**Question 18**
• division	• division	• shapes
• solids	• money	• probability

ISBN: 978-1-77149-201-0

⑲ Rachel picked a marble randomly from a bag and put it back. She used a bar graph to show the number of times each colour was picked. What is the chance of Rachel picking a marble that is not red on her next try?

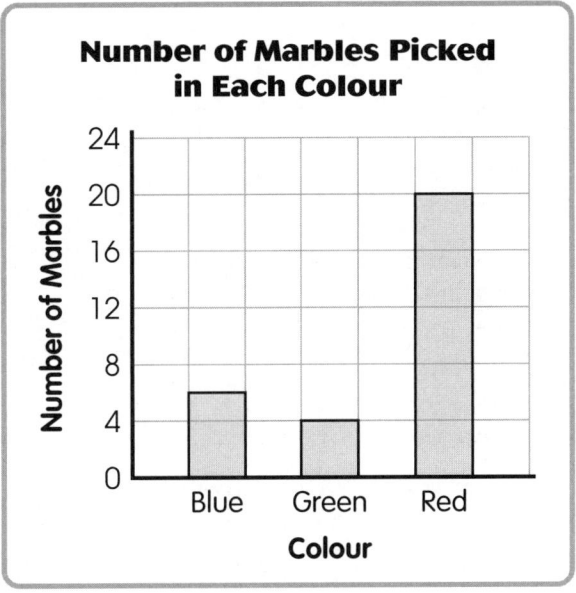

⑳ The pictograph shows the amount of time each child spent on exercising. How many more minutes did the girls spend on exercising than the boys?

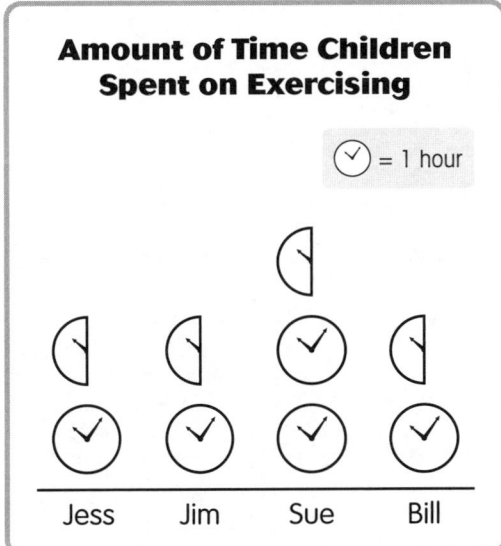

Topics covered:

Question 19
- data management
- probability

Question 20
- addition
- time
- data management

ISBN: 978-1-77149-201-0

Students are required to solve multi-step questions which involve various topics in each.

Topics Covered

	Number Sense and Numeration	Measurement	Geometry and Spatial Sense	Patterning and Algebra	Data Management and Probability	My Record ✔ correct ✗ incorrect
1	multiplication division	time				
2	division fractions					
3	multiplication money					
4	multiplication	mass				
5		perimeter	shapes			
6	addition	capacity				
7	multiplication money					
8			solids		data management	
9		area	locations	patterning		
10	division	mass				
11		perimeter		patterning		
12	division	perimeter				
13	money				probability	
14	fractions	time				
15		time capacity				
16					probability / data management	
17	subtraction	mass			data management	
18	fractions			patterning		
19	division		solids			
20		perimeter	shapes			

ISBN: 978-1-77149-201-0

① A light flashes 4 times every 6 seconds. How many times does it flash in 1 minute?

Number of "6 seconds" in 1 minute: _____ ÷ _____ = _____

Number of times it flashes: _____ × _____ = _____

The light flashes _____ .

② Benjamin has 6 cakes. He divides the cakes evenly among 36 friends. What fraction of a cake does each friend get?

Hints

How many pieces will 1 cake be divided into?

③ Ronnie wants to buy 8 candies. Each candy costs 10¢. If Ronnie pays with a toonie, what will his change be?

④ Each reference book weighs 2000 g. How many kilograms is a set of 6 reference books?

Topics covered:

Question 1	Question 2	Question 3	Question 4
• multiplication	• division	• multiplication	• multiplication
• division	• fractions	• money	• mass
• time			

ISBN: 978-1-77149-201-0

⑤ A square wooden board with a side length of 12 cm is cut into 4 identical squares. What is the perimeter of each small piece?

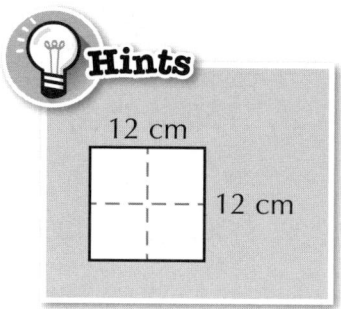

⑥ There are 8 ice cubes in a glass of water. Each ice cube melts into 9 mL of water. If the glass already has 350 mL of water, how many millilitres of water will there be after all the ice cubes melt?

⑦ A basket of tomatoes costs $3.48 and a bag of broccoli costs $2.52. How much do 7 baskets of tomatoes and 7 bags of broccoli cost?

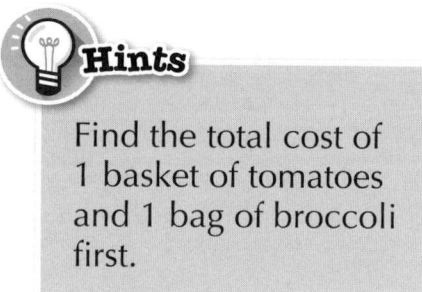

Find the total cost of 1 basket of tomatoes and 1 bag of broccoli first.

Topics covered:

Question 5	**Question 6**	**Question 7**
• perimeter	• addition	• multiplication
• shapes	• capacity	• money

ISBN: 978-1-77149-201-0

⑧ The pictograph shows the blocks in Jake's toy box. He wants to paint all the faces on his cubes and triangular pyramids. How many faces does he have to paint?

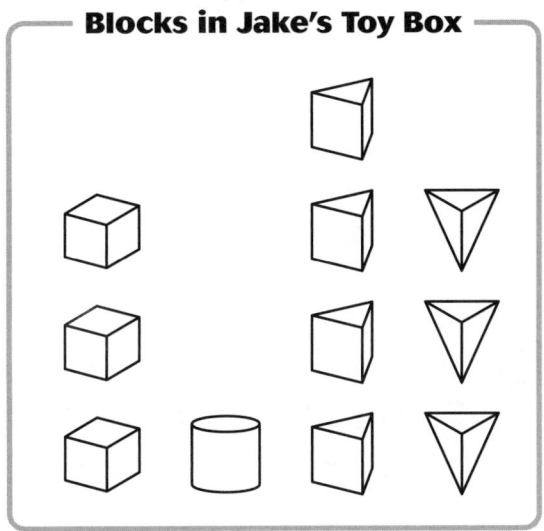

Blocks in Jake's Toy Box

⑨ A park is being built in 5 phases. B2 and C2 are completed in Phase 1, B3 and C3 in Phase 2, and B4 and C4 in Phase 3. If the pattern continues, what is the area of the park?

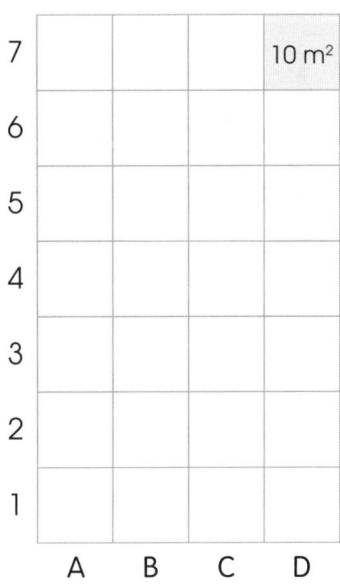

Topics covered:

Question 8
- solids
- data management

Question 9
- area
- locations
- patterning

ISBN: 978-1-77149-201-0

⑩ Jason has bought 4 bags of flour that weigh 28 kg in total. How many grams does 1 bag of flour weigh?

⑪ Farmer Rick's chicken pen measures 2 m by 1 m in Year 1, 3 m by 2 m in Year 2, and 4 m by 3 m in Year 3. What will the perimeter of the chicken pen be by Year 5?

⑫ 4 small squares of the same size are put together to form a large square. The side length of the large square is 8 cm. What is the perimeter of a small square?

**Hints**

Make a sketch of the large square first.

Topics covered:

Question 10	**Question 11**	**Question 12**
• division	• perimeter	• division
• mass	• patterning	• perimeter

ISBN: 978-1-77149-201-0

⑬ There are 4 envelopes each with $20 in bills. The number of bills in each envelope are not the same. What is the chance of picking an envelope with a $20 bill?

Hints

Find all the ways to make $20 using only bills.

⑭ In a 20-minute training session, Cathy spent $\frac{1}{10}$ of it on warming up, $\frac{4}{5}$ on running, and the remaining time on resting. How long did she rest for? Write your answer as a fraction in hours.

⑮ Sam started catching water dripping at 11:35 using a 2-L bucket. The bucket was filled by 12:20. Sam emptied the bucket each time it was full. By what time had Sam emptied out a total of 8000 mL of water?

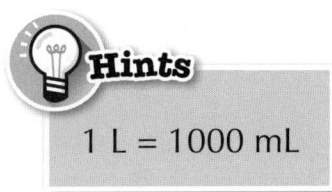

Hints

1 L = 1000 mL

Topics covered:

Question 13	**Question 14**	**Question 15**
• money	• fractions	• time
• probability	• time	• capacity

ISBN: 978-1-77149-201-0

⑯ The pictograph shows the different coloured beads Amy has in a bag. How many green and yellow beads are there? What is the chance of Amy picking a green or a yellow bead?

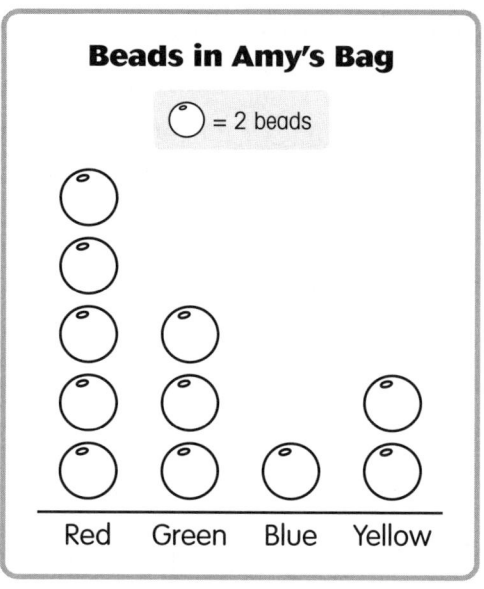

Beads in Amy's Bag

◯ = 2 beads

Red   Green   Blue   Yellow

⑰ The bar graph shows how much each animal weighs. Which is heavier, a tiger or a lion? How much heavier?

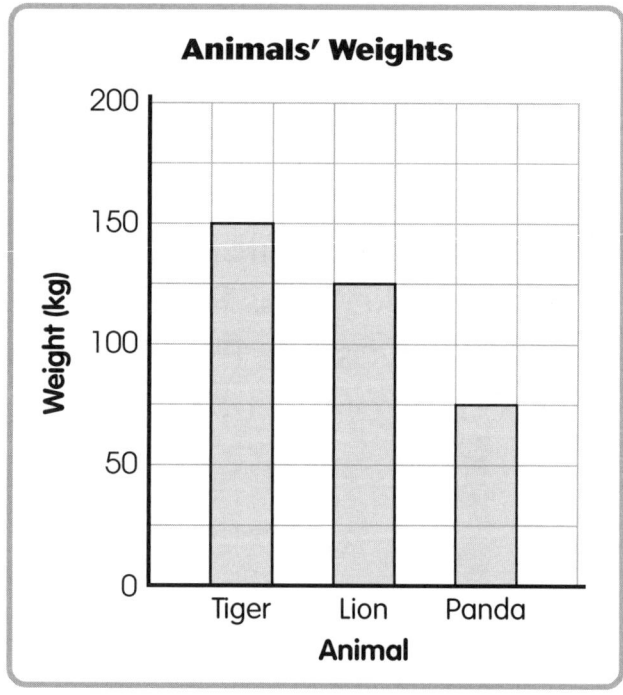

Animals' Weights

Topics covered:

Question 16
• probability
• data management

Question 17
• subtraction
• mass
• data management

ISBN: 978-1-77149-201-0

⑱ Jazz makes 3 pizzas in $\frac{1}{2}$ h, 6 pizzas in 1 h, and 9 pizzas in $1\frac{1}{2}$ h. If the pattern continues, how many pizzas can she make in 2 h?

⑲ Gary wants to make a triangular prism with edges that have the same length. He cuts up a 63-cm stick to make the edges. How long will each edge be?

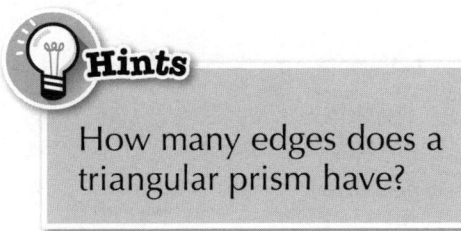

Hints

How many edges does a triangular prism have?

⑳ Jane has 2 squares that both have a side length of 10 cm. Jane combines the 2 squares to make a rectangle. She thinks the perimeter of the rectangle is equal to the perimeter of the two squares added together. Is she correct?

Topics covered:

Question 18	**Question 19**	**Question 20**
• fractions	• division	• perimeter
• patterning	• solids	• shapes

ISBN: 978-1-77149-201-0

 Students are required to solve multi-step questions which involve various topics in each.

Topics Covered

	Number Sense and Numeration	Measurement	Geometry and Spatial Sense	Patterning and Algebra	Data Management and Probability	My Record ✔ correct ✘ incorrect
1	division	perimeter				
2	fractions	time				
3	multiplication	time				
4	subtraction	capacity				
5	fractions	perimeter				
6	division money	time				
7	addition division	capacity				
8	multiplication				data management	
9		time temperature		patterning	data management	
10	multiplication division					
11	fractions	capacity time				
12	division		solids			
13	money				probability	
14	multiplication	area	solids			
15	decimals			patterning		
16		perimeter	shapes			
17	division			patterning		
18	multiplication				probability	
19	multiplication	area				
20		area	locations movements			

ISBN: 978-1-77149-201-0

① Amanda places 6 cards of the same size on a scrapbook page that measures 12 cm by 10 cm. What is the perimeter of 1 card?

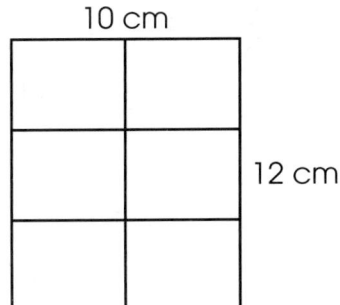

Length of 1 card: 10 ÷ _____ = _____

Width of 1 card: 12 ÷ _____ = _____

Perimeter: _____ + _____ + _____ + _____ = _____

The perimeter of 1 card is _____ .

② At Lakeview Public School, classes start at 9:00 and finish at 3:00. Of that time, $\frac{5}{6}$ of it is spent in class and the rest is for recess. How many minutes of recess do the students at Lakeview Public School get each day?

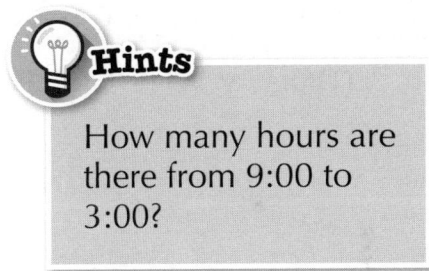

Hints

How many hours are there from 9:00 to 3:00?

③ Perry has to complete 2 sheets that each have 5 math questions. It takes him 3 minutes to complete 1 question. If he starts at 12:45, what time will he finish all of the math questions?

Topics covered:

Question 1	**Question 2**	**Question 3**
• division	• fractions	• multiplication
• perimeter	• time	• time

ISBN: 978-1-77149-201-0

④ Cassidy has 2 L of water. Meredith has 1875 mL. Who has more water and by how many more millilitres?

⑤ Mr. Collins's backyard is 8 m in length and 6 m in width. His inflated pool is $\frac{1}{4}$ of the length and $\frac{1}{2}$ of the width of his backyard. What is the perimeter of his pool?

⑥ Jake saves 1 loonie and 2 quarters each week. How much money will he have in 21 days?

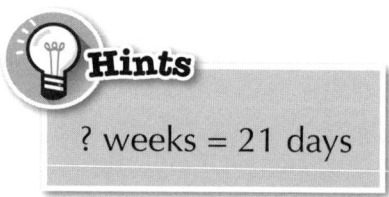

Hints

? weeks = 21 days

⑦ 27 L of cranberry juice is divided equally into 9 bottles. How many millilitres of juice is there in 2 bottles?

Topics covered:

Question 4	**Question 5**	**Question 6**	**Question 7**
• subtraction	• fractions	• division	• addition
• capacity	• perimeter	• money	• division
		• time	• capacity

ISBN: 978-1-77149-201-0

⑧ The pictograph shows the number of vases there are for each vase size. There are 3 flowers in a small vase, 10 in a medium vase, and 20 in a large vase. How many flowers are there in all?

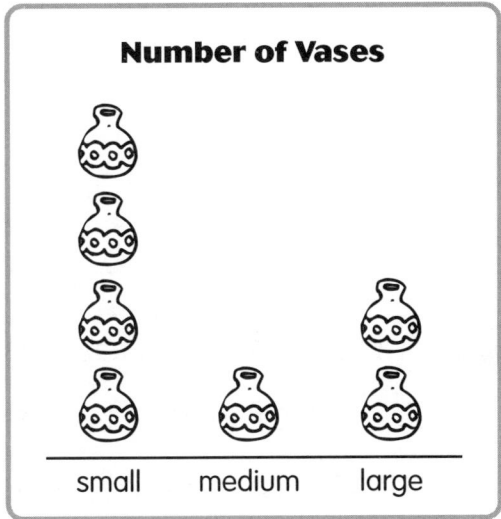

Number of Vases

small   medium   large

⑨ The bar graph shows the temperature of Isaac's drink at different times. If the pattern continues, when will his drink be 25°C?

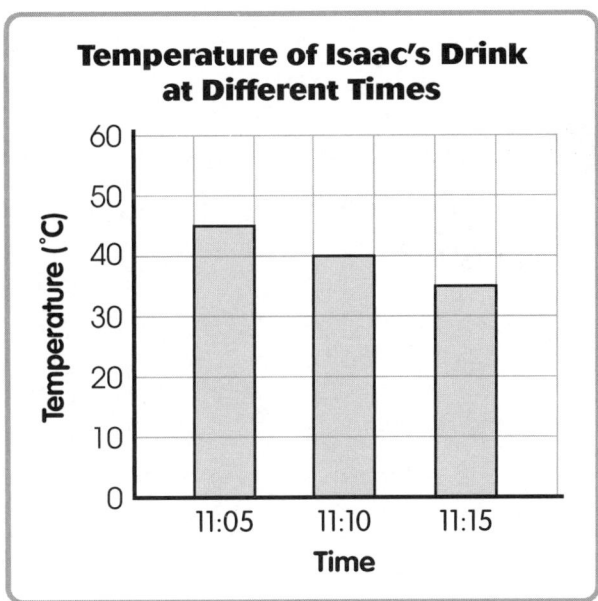

Topics covered:

Question 8
- multiplication
- data management

Question 9
- time
- temperature
- patterning
- data management

ISBN: 978-1-77149-201-0

⑩ 72 students went to the zoo. They were divided into groups of 8. 3 groups went to see giraffes. How many students went to see giraffes?

⑪ A bucket that has a capacity of 20 L is $\frac{1}{2}$ full. The faucet adds 2 litres of water to the bucket every 5 minutes. If the faucet is turned on at 4:45, what time will the bucket be full?

⑫ Jacob has 2 sticks that are 24 cm each. He cuts them up to make a square-based prism. How long are the edges of the prism?

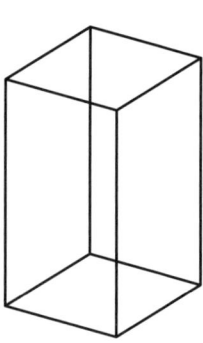

Topics covered:

Question 10	**Question 11**	**Question 12**
• multiplication	• fractions	• division
• division	• capacity	• solids
	• time	

ISBN: 978-1-77149-201-0

⑬ Melissa had $7.85 in the fewest coins in her pocket but she accidentally dropped one of them. What was the chance that the lost coin was a nickel?

⑭ Alice wants to make a triangular prism. The area of each rectangular face is twice that of a triangular face. If the area of each triangular face is 5 cm², what is the total area of the rectangular faces?

⑮ A loaf of bread was cut into 10 slices. A total of 2 slices had been eaten by Day 1, 3 by Day 2, and 4 by Day 3. If this pattern continued, how much of the loaf was left after Day 6? Write your answer as a decimal.

Topics covered:

Question 13	Question 14	Question 15
• money	• multiplication	• decimals
• probability	• area	• patterning
	• solids	

ISBN: 978-1-77149-201-0

⑯ Jessie has a 4-sided shape that measures 4 cm on two sides. Its perimeter is 16 cm. Can it be a square? Explain.

⑰ Teresa records the number of quarters she earns each week. Write the pattern rule. How much will she earn in Week 4?

Teresa's Earnings

Week	Number of Quarters
1	2
2	4
3	8

⑱ Each sack has 6 marbles. Olivia bought 4 sacks of blue marbles, 1 sack green, and 5 sacks yellow. How many marbles are there in total? If Olivia empties all sacks into a bag, what is her chance of picking a green marble?

Topics covered:

Question 16
• perimeter
• shapes

Question 17
• division
• patterning

Question 18
• multiplication
• probability

ISBN: 978-1-77149-201-0

⑲ Ms. Jean's old rug is 2 m in length and 1 m in width. She has bought a new rug that is 2 times the length and 3 times the width of her old rug. How much greater is the area of the new rug?

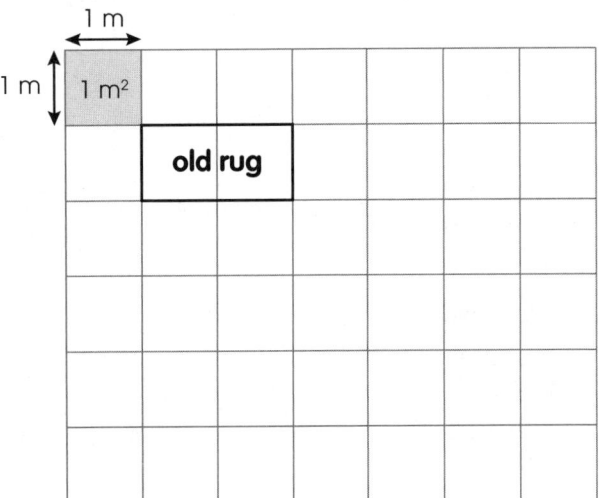

⑳ A stamp is on B4 and C4. Andy makes a design by sliding the stamp 2 squares down and 2 squares to the right. Name the squares that the design covers. What is the area of the design?

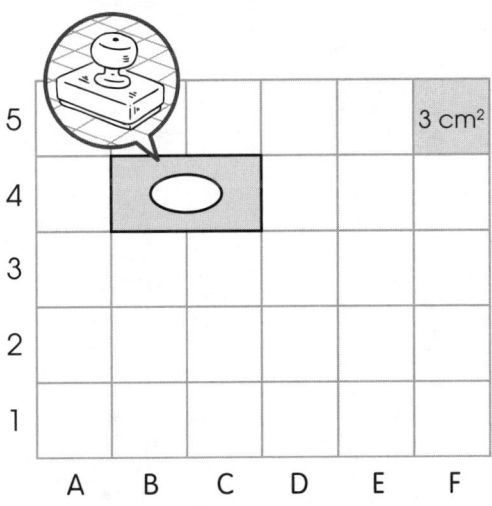

 **Hints**

Look at the grid closely to find the area of each square.

Topics covered:

Question 19
- multiplication
- area

Question 20
- area
- locations
- movements

ISBN: 978-1-77149-201-0

Students are required to solve multi-step questions which involve various topics in each.

Topics Covered

	Number Sense and Numeration	Measurement	Geometry and Spatial Sense	Patterning and Algebra	Data Management and Probability	My Record ✔ correct ✗ incorrect
1	addition multiplication					☐
2	addition subtraction					☐
3	division money		solids			☐
4		area	locations movements			☐
5	subtraction				data management	☐
6		perimeter	solids			☐
7	addition money					☐
8		perimeter	shapes			☐
9	subtraction division					☐
10	fractions				probability	☐
11	addition	time				☐
12		temperature		patterning		☐
13	fractions		solids		probability	☐
14		perimeter	shapes			☐
15	decimals	mass				☐
16		area	locations movements			☐
17	money				data management	☐
18	addition	capacity		patterning		☐
19	addition division					☐
20	money			patterning		☐

ISBN: 978-1-77149-201-0

① Shannon picked 238 grapes yesterday. Today, she picked 8 bunches of grapes, each with 10 grapes. How many grapes does she have in all?

② On Friday, a library had 2079 books. Over the weekend, 497 books were returned and 310 books were lent out. How many books does the library have now?

③ Jackie built a triangular prism using wooden boards. Each triangular board cost $5.25 and the total cost of all boards was $34.50. How much did each rectangular board cost?

Topics covered:

Question 1	Question 2	Question 3
• addition	• addition	• division
• multiplication	• subtraction	• money
		• solids

ISBN: 978-1-77149-201-0

④ The school janitor rotated the desk $\frac{1}{4}$ counterclockwise about Point A. How many square metres of the rug is now below the desk?

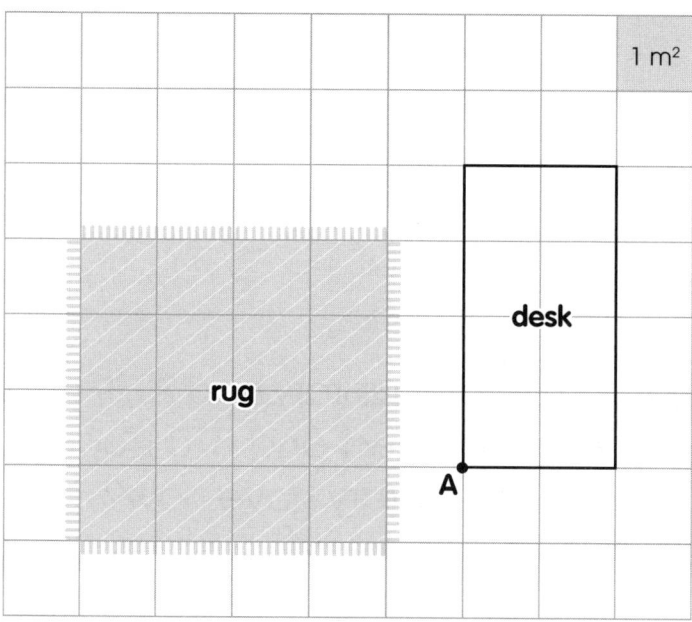

⑤ The pictograph shows the number of books the children have read. How many more books have the boys read than the girls?

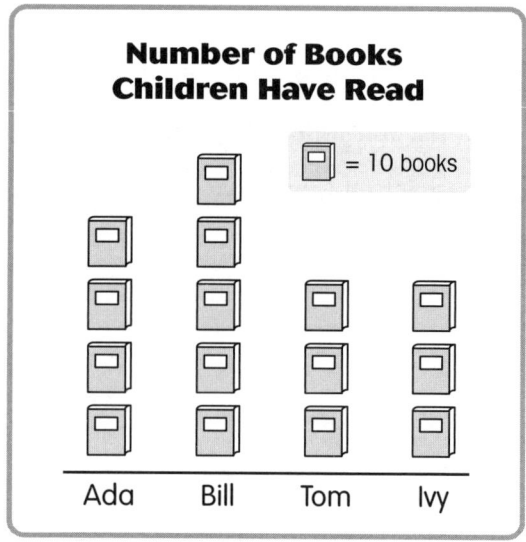

**Number of Books
Children Have Read**

= 10 books

| Ada | Bill | Tom | Ivy |

Topics covered:

Question 4
- area
- locations
- movements

Question 5
- subtraction
- data management

ISBN: 978-1-77149-201-0

⑥ What is the perimeter of the net? What solid does the net form?

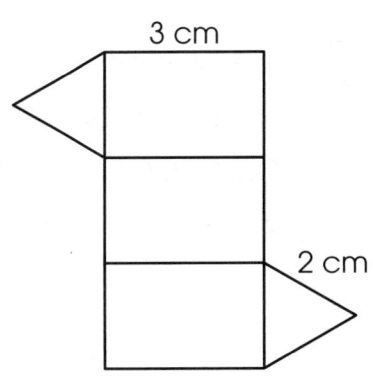

⑦ Ron has 4 toonies, 4 quarters, and 4 dimes. Marvin has twice as many toonies, quarters, and dimes that Ron has. How much does Marvin have left after buying a $15 T-shirt?

⑧ Grayson builds a rhombus-shaped frame using a 36-cm strip of wood. What is the side length of the frame?

⑨ Cory had 112 stickers. After giving some of them to Anna and Tom, he now has 94 stickers left. If Cory gave the same number of stickers to Anna and Tom, how many stickers did each of them get?

Topics covered:

Question 6	Question 7	Question 8	Question 9
• perimeter	• addition	• perimeter	• subtraction
• solids	• money	• shapes	• division

⑩ A spinner is divided into 12 equal parts. Each part is either red, blue, or green. It is equally likely that the spinner will land on blue or on green. How much of the spinner is red at most? Write your answer as a fraction.

⑪ Mr. Smith drove 130 minutes to a campsite. On his way back, he drove an additional 30 minutes due to traffic. How much time did Mr. Smith spend on driving? Write your answer in hours and minutes.

⑫ Ms. Lane's furnace broke down. The temperatures were 24°C at 1:00, 23°C at 1:15, and 22°C at 1:30. If the pattern continued, what time would the temperature be 20°C?

Topics covered:

Question 10	**Question 11**	**Question 12**
• fractions	• addition	• temperature
• probability	• time	• patterning

ISBN: 978-1-77149-201-0

⑬ Carl is painting a wooden cube. He has painted all its faces except the bottom one. Write a fraction to represent the painted faces of the cube. If he rolls this cube, what is the chance of getting the unpainted face?

⑭ A shape has 4 sides. One pair of sides measures 24 cm each and another pair measures 12 cm each. Find its perimeter. Fred thinks it must be a rectangle. Is he correct? If not, what other shapes can it be?

⑮ A pumpkin weighs 10 kg. A honeydew's weight is 0.4 of the pumpkin's. How many more grams does the pumpkin weigh than the honeydew?

Topics covered:

Question 13	**Question 14**	**Question 15**
• fractions	• perimeter	• decimals
• solids	• shapes	• mass
• probability		

ISBN: 978-1-77149-201-0

⑯ Hannah transformed a shape to create a design. Identify the transformation. If the pattern continued, what would the area of the design be after 2 more transformations?

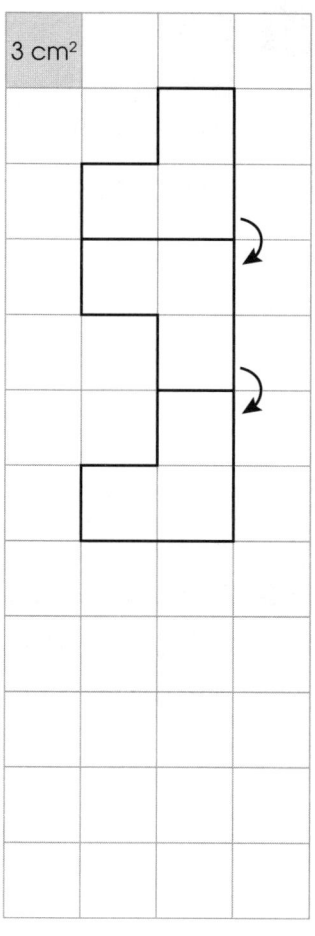

⑰ The bar graph shows the number of each type of coin Cooper has in his piggy bank. If Jane has $10, how much more money does Jane have than Cooper?

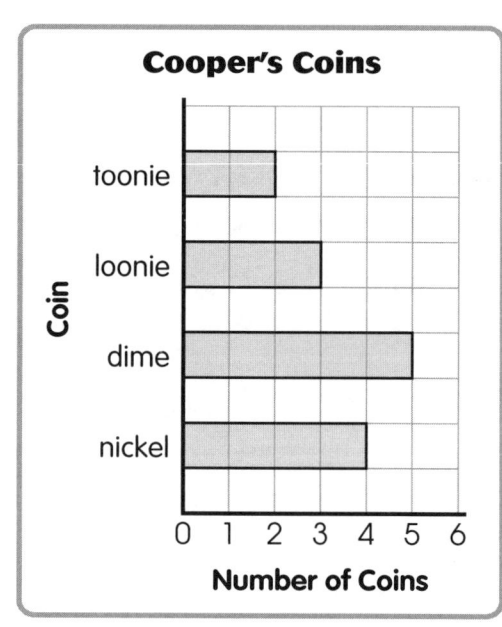

Topics covered:

Question 16	Question 17
• area	• money
• locations	• data management
• movements	

ISBN: 978-1-77149-201-0

⑱ A bucket that has a capacity of 4 L was left outside during the rain. There was 500 mL of water in the bucket after 30 min, 1 L after 60 min, and 1500 mL after 90 min. How many minutes did it take for the bucket to be half full?

⑲ A furniture factory needs to build 400 desks. 392 have already been built. A desk needs 4 legs. Will 28 legs be enough to build the remaining desks?

⑳ Rachel had $20.75. She had spent 2 toonies by Monday, 4 toonies by Tuesday, and 6 toonies by Wednesday. If the pattern continued, how much was left after Friday?

Topics covered:

Question 18	**Question 19**	**Question 20**
• addition	• addition	• money
• capacity	• division	• patterning
• patterning		

Students are required to solve multi-step questions which involve various topics in each.

Topics Covered

	Number Sense and Numeration	Measurement	Geometry and Spatial Sense	Patterning and Algebra	Data Management and Probability	My Record ✔ correct ✘ incorrect
1	addition	capacity				☐
2	division	perimeter	shapes			☐
3	fractions	perimeter				☐
4	division		solids			☐
5	multiplication fractions					☐
6	subtraction	time				☐
7	fractions decimals	temperature				☐
8		perimeter	shapes			☐
9	multiplication			patterning		☐
10		area	locations movements			☐
11		time		patterning		☐
12	addition	mass				☐
13	division	mass				☐
14	money			patterning		☐
15	addition subtraction					☐
16					probability / data management	☐
17			solids		data management	☐
18	fractions decimals				probability	☐
19	fractions	time				☐
20	subtraction multiplication					☐

ISBN: 978-1-77149-201-0

① A bottle has 500 mL. If Craig drinks 6 bottles of water, how many litres of water does he drink?

② Zach drew a square and a triangle. The side lengths of both shapes are identical. If the sum of their perimeters is 63 cm, what is the perimeter of each shape?

③ Mr. Jackson is reducing the size of his garden. His fence currently measures 12 m in length and 6 m in width. If the new garden is $\frac{1}{3}$ of the length and $\frac{1}{2}$ of the width, what will the perimeter of the new garden be?

Topics covered:

Question 1	**Question 2**	**Question 3**
• addition	• division	• fractions
• capacity	• perimeter	• perimeter
	• shapes	

ISBN: 978-1-77149-201-0

④ Andy cut a 54-cm stick into equal pieces to build solids. He constructed a triangular pyramid. If he constructed a triangular prism instead, how much shorter would each stick be?

⑤ There are 20 houses on a street. $\frac{1}{5}$ of the houses have 2 residents, $\frac{2}{5}$ of them have 3 residents, and $\frac{2}{5}$ of them have 4 residents. How many residents are there in all?

⑥ A movie is 1 hour and 57 minutes long. Anthony watched it for 37 minutes, fast-forwarded 5 minutes of it, and then watched for another 47 minutes. How many minutes of the movie is left?

Topics covered:

Question 4	**Question 5**	**Question 6**
• division	• multiplication	• subtraction
• solids	• fractions	• time

ISBN: 978-1-77149-201-0

⑦ One day, it was 10°C in Tokyo, Japan. The temperature in Vancouver, Canada was 0.5 that of Tokyo, and the temperature in London, England was $\frac{3}{5}$ that of Tokyo. How much warmer was it in London than in Vancouver?

⑧ A triangle is shown below. William uses 2 triangles to make a square. What is the perimeter of the square?

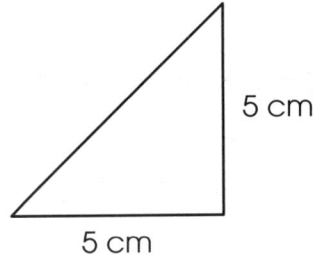

5 cm

5 cm

⑨ The mass of a pumpkin is 2 kg in Week 1, 3 kg in Week 2, and 4 kg in Week 3. If the pattern continues, what is the total mass of 6 pumpkins in Week 5 if they have the same mass?

Topics covered:

Question 7
- fractions
- decimals
- temperature

Question 8
- perimeter
- shapes

Question 9
- multiplication
- patterning

ISBN: 978-1-77149-201-0

⑩ Craig painted B2, B3, C2, and C3 on the grid below. He then folded the grid along Line Y before the paint dried. Colour the painted squares on the grid. What is the area of the painted shape?

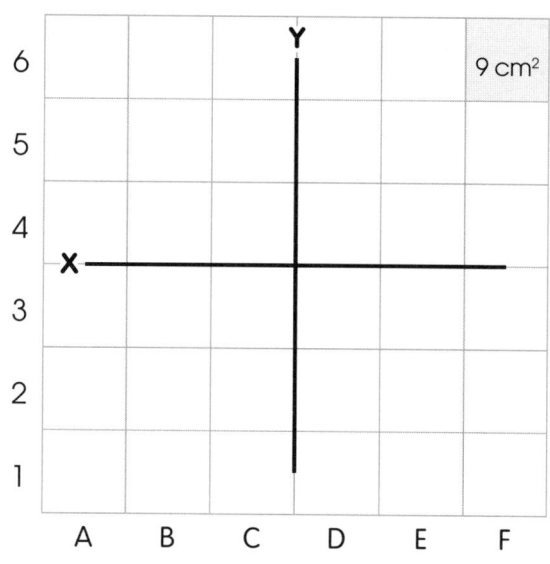

9 cm²

⑪ Karen had soccer practice every 2 days and drawing lessons every 4 days. Both activities started on September 1. How many days did Karen have both activities on the same day in September?

September 2016						
Sun	Mon	Tue	Wed	Thu	Fri	Sat
				1	2	3
4	5	6	7	8	9	10
11	12	13	14	15	16	17
18	19	20	21	22	23	24
25	26	27	28	29	30	

Topics covered:

Question 10
- area
- locations
- movements

Question 11
- time
- patterning

ISBN: 978-1-77149-201-0

⑫ A rope can carry a mass of 8 kg at most. If Jason plans to use the rope to hang 20 sweaters that weigh 500 g each, will the rope break?

⑬ A 24-kg box of potatoes is divided into 6 sacks. How many grams does 1 sack weigh?

⑭ Rebecca has $5.95 in coins in her pocket. She has the fewest coins possible. She dropped one of the coins. What is the chance that the coin has a value greater than 50¢?

⑮ There were 1023 people at a mall. 228 people have left and 153 people have arrived. How many people are at the mall now?

Topics covered:

Question 12	Question 13	Question 14	Question 15
• addition	• division	• money	• addition
• mass	• mass	• patterning	• subtraction

⑯ The bar graph shows the number of cards of each colour drawn from a deck. How many red and blue cards were drawn? Based on the results, what is the chance of drawing a red or blue card?

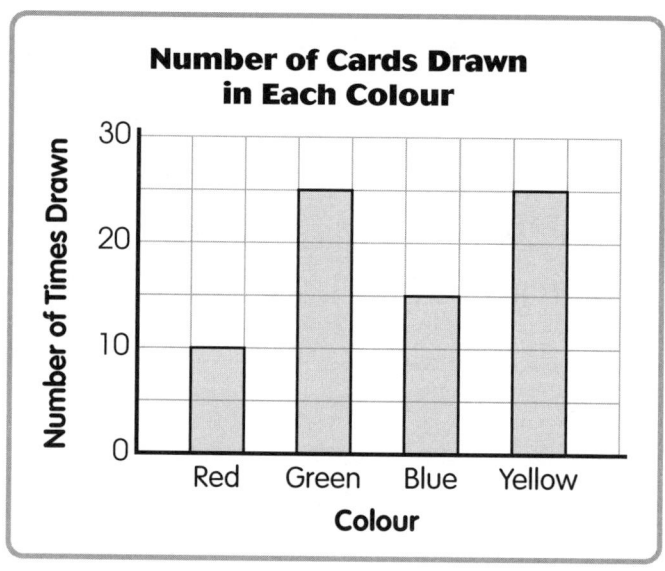

Number of Cards Drawn in Each Colour

⑰ The pictograph shows the different solids in Lennox's toy box. Which solids have more than 4 faces? How many of them are there?

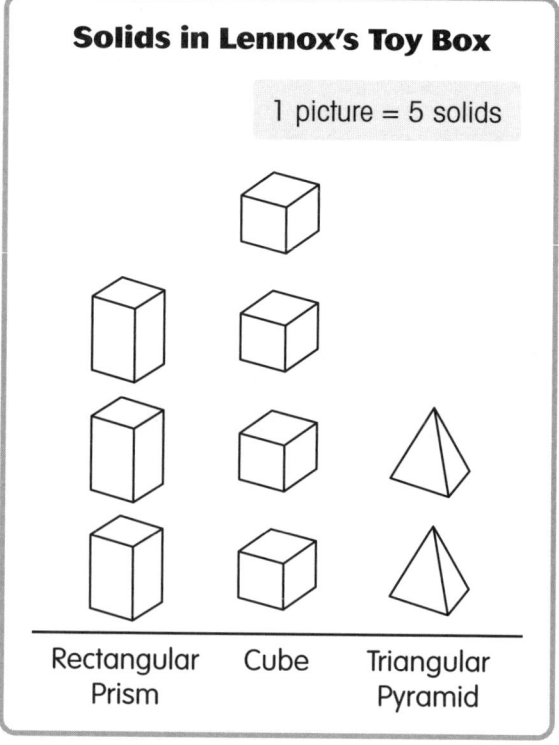

Solids in Lennox's Toy Box

1 picture = 5 solids

Topics covered:

Question 16
- probability
- data management

Question 17
- solids
- data management

ISBN: 978-1-77149-201-0

⑱ A box has 2 blue, 10 green, and 6 red marbles. If Vincent takes out $\frac{1}{2}$ of the blue marbles and 0.5 of the green marbles, and then picks a marble randomly, what is his chance of picking a green marble?

⑲ The Lee family bought 3 apple pies. Each pie is cut into 8 equal pieces. If the family eats $\frac{3}{8}$ of a pie each day, how much pie will be left after a week? Write your answer as a fraction.

⑳ Of the 120 horses on Mr. Liam's ranch, 113 of them do not need their horseshoes replaced. If 1 horse requires 4 horseshoes, how many horseshoes does Mr. Liam need to replace?

Topics covered:

Question 18	**Question 19**	**Question 20**
• fractions	• fractions	• subtraction
• decimals	• time	• multiplication
• probability		

ISBN: 978-1-77149-201-0

8 Students are required to solve multi-step questions which involve various topics in each.

Topics Covered

	Number Sense and Numeration	Measurement	Geometry and Spatial Sense	Patterning and Algebra	Data Management and Probability	My Record ✔ correct ✘ incorrect
1	multiplication				data management	
2		area	locations movements			
3	addition	capacity				
4			solids		probability	
5	multiplication fractions	time				
6	multiplication	mass				
7	addition	perimeter				
8	subtraction money					
9		time temperature		patterning		
10	subtraction	mass				
11	fractions				probability	
12	multiplication	perimeter	shapes			
13			solids		probability	
14	multiplication division					
15	multiplication money					
16	subtraction			patterning		
17	fractions	capacity				
18	money			patterning		
19	fractions				data management	
20			solids locations			

ISBN: 978-1-77149-201-0

① The pictograph shows the number of goals each soccer player scored in a season. How many goals were scored in all?

Number of Goals Scored

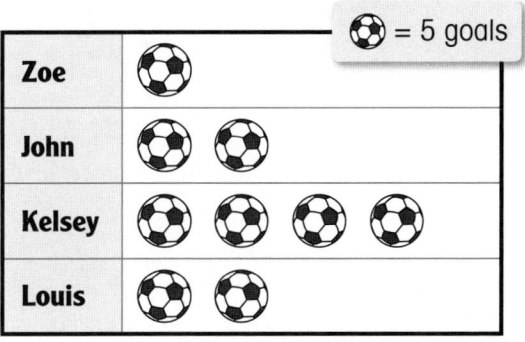

② Chester is laying a stone path. The stone path starts at B1 and then goes 5 squares up and 3 squares to the right. What is the area covered by the stone path?

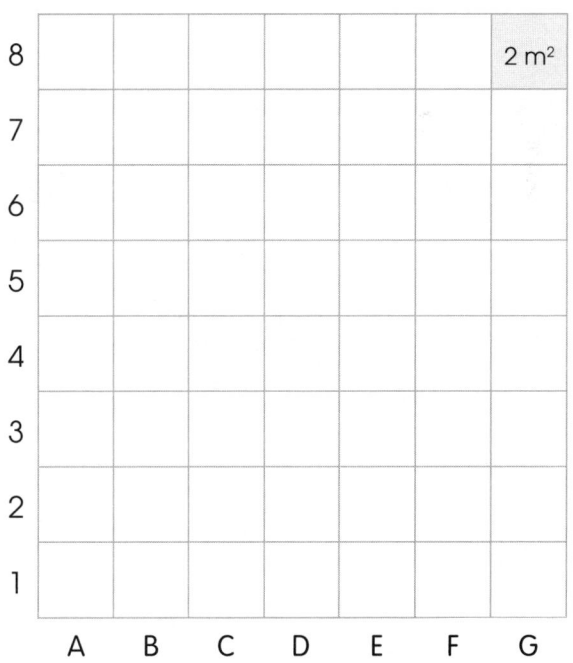

Topics covered:

Question 1
- multiplication
- data management

Question 2
- area
- locations
- movements

ISBN: 978-1-77149-201-0

③ Tony spilled 450 mL of milk on the floor accidentally. Now there is only 2 L of milk left in the carton. How many mL of milk was in the carton before Tony spilled it?

④ Justin takes 2 square-based pyramids and glues the square faces together. He then paints 3 of the faces and tosses the solid. What is the chance of it landing on a face that is not painted?

⑤ Oscar has two sheets of paper that each have 6 math problems. If Oscar starts working at 12:45 and spends 5 minutes on each math problem, what time will he complete $1\frac{1}{2}$ of the math problems?

Topics covered:		
Question 3	**Question 4**	**Question 5**
• addition	• solids	• multiplication
• capacity	• probability	• fractions
		• time

ISBN: 978-1-77149-201-0

⑥ A 6-kg box is on one end of the scale. How many 500-g blocks are needed to balance the scale?

⑦ Simone wants to frame a painting that measures 50 cm by 30 cm. The frame is 10 cm longer than the painting on all sides. What is the perimeter of the frame?

⑧ Lawrence has three $10 bills. He uses them to buy a $24.75 present for his mom. What will Lawrence's change be in the fewest bills and coins?

⑨ The temperature of a drink dropped by 2°C every 5 minutes. If the drink was 50°C at first, what was the temperature of the drink after half an hour?

Topics covered:

Question 6	**Question 7**	**Question 8**	**Question 9**
• multiplication	• addition	• subtraction	• time
• mass	• perimeter	• money	• temperature
			• patterning

ISBN: 978-1-77149-201-0

⑩ Mr. Robin bought 8 kg of soil. He used 2500 g for his front yard and 5 kg for his backyard. If Mr. Robin needs at least 675 g for his indoor plants, does he have enough soil?

⑪ $\frac{1}{5}$ of a spinner is red, $\frac{2}{5}$ is green, and the rest is blue. What is the chance of the arrow not landing on blue?

⑫ Justin is making stars with yarn. Each star is made up of 2 overlapping triangles as shown. Measure the sides with a ruler. Will 50 cm of yarn be enough to make 3 stars?

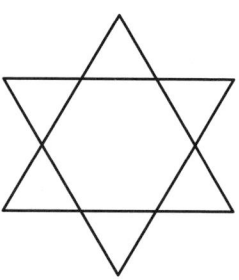

Topics covered:

Question 10	**Question 11**	**Question 12**
• subtraction	• fractions	• multiplication
• mass	• probability	• perimeter
		• shapes

ISBN: 978-1-77149-201-0

⑬ Allen has a total of 10 cones and rectangular prisms in a bag. The chance of picking a solid that can slide and be stacked is likely. How many rectangular prisms could there be?

⑭ Tracy baked 3 trays of 8 cookies. She gives them away equally to 6 friends. How many cookies does each friend get?

⑮ Thomas has $8 in loonies and quarters. How many quarters could he have at most?

Topics covered:

Question 13	**Question 14**	**Question 15**
• solids	• multiplication	• multiplication
• probability	• division	• money

⑯ Leanne had 754 beads for making bracelets. She had 729 beads left after making 1 bracelet and 704 beads left after making 2 bracelets. How many beads were left after she had made 3 more bracelets?

⑰ Jason's container is only $\frac{1}{2}$ full. If there is 1500 mL of water in the container, what is the capacity of the container in litres?

⑱ Oscar has 9 loonies and 9 dimes after Day 1, 8 loonies and 8 dimes after Day 2, and 7 loonies and 7 dimes after Day 3. If the pattern continues, how much will he have after Day 6?

Topics covered:

Question 16	**Question 17**	**Question 18**
• subtraction	• fractions	• money
• patterning	• capacity	• patterning

ISBN: 978-1-77149-201-0

⑲ The graph shows the children's favourite bakery items. $\frac{1}{2}$ as many children who voted pie voted for muffin; $\frac{2}{3}$ as many children who voted muffin voted for cookie. Complete the bar graph. How many children voted in all?

⑳ Jackie drew the net below. Before making the solid, she coloured the top and she wants to colour the bottom as well. Write the coordinates of the squares she should colour. Then name the solid that the net makes.

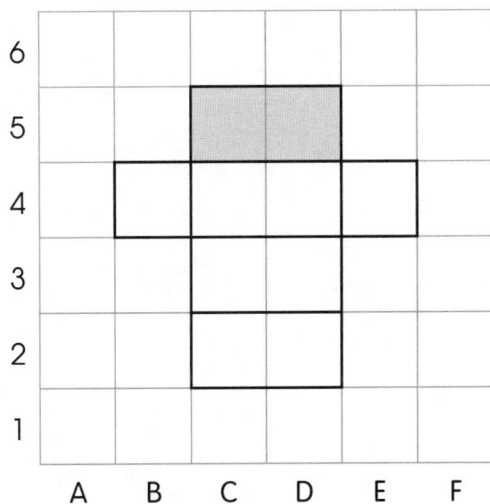

Topics covered:

Question 19
- fractions
- data management

Question 20
- solids
- locations

ISBN: 978-1-77149-201-0

Students are required to solve multi-step questions which involve various topics in each.

Topics Covered

	Number Sense and Numeration	Measurement	Geometry and Spatial Sense	Patterning and Algebra	Data Management and Probability	My Record ✔ correct ✗ incorrect
1	fractions decimals				probability	
2	subtraction multiplication	capacity				
3	multiplication money					
4	time			patterning		
5	division money					
6		perimeter	shapes			
7	division	mass				
8		temperature			data management	
9	addition	capacity			data management	
10	multiplication		solids			
11	multiplication		solids			
12		temperature		patterning		
13	multiplication	capacity				
14	fractions decimals				probability	
15	subtraction division					
16		area	locations movements			
17			locations movements	patterning		
18	fractions				probability	
19		perimeter	shapes			
20		area	solids			

ISBN: 978-1-77149-201-0

① Shelby bought a pack of 20 juice boxes. 0.1 of them are apple juice, $\frac{3}{10}$ of them are cranberry juice, and the rest are orange juice. If she picks a juice box randomly, what is her chance of picking orange juice?

② Connor needed to take 10 mL of medicine each day for 10 days. If the bottle had 350 mL of medicine, how much medicine was left after 10 days?

③ Jason paid $30 for 3 toys that each cost $6 and a book that cost $4.45. If the cashier ran out of quarters, what would Jason's change be in the fewest bills and coins?

Topics covered:

Question 1	**Question 2**	**Question 3**
• fractions	• subtraction	• multiplication
• decimals	• multiplication	• money
• probability	• capacity	

④ A bell rings at 1:15, 1:30, and 1:45. If the pattern continues, will the bell ring at 2:20?

⑤ Toy trains cost $8.75 each and toy cars cost $6.25 each. If Joseph spent exactly $50 on 1 toy train, 1 toy car, and 5 books, how much did each book cost?

⑥ Alyssa made a large rectangle by putting 8 squares together. The rectangle is 4 squares long and 2 squares wide. If the side length of each square is 20 cm, what is the perimeter of the rectangle?

⑦ A 42-kg piece of wood was cut into 7 equal pieces. How much did a single piece weigh in grams?

Topics covered:			
Question 4	**Question 5**	**Question 6**	**Question 7**
• time	• division	• perimeter	• division
• patterning	• money	• shapes	• mass

  ISBN: 978-1-77149-201-0

⑧ The graph below shows the temperatures last week. Which 2 consecutive days showed the greatest change in temperature? What was the difference?

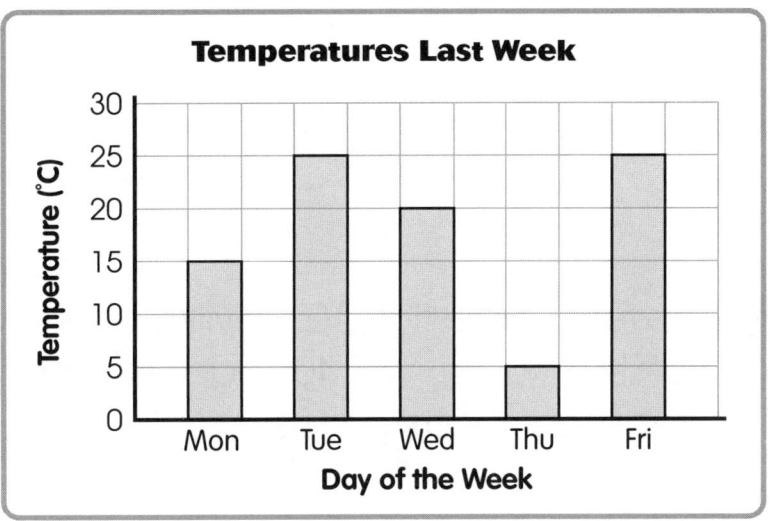

⑨ The bar graph shows how much water there is in each container. Can a bottle with a capacity of 1 L be completely filled with water from these containers?

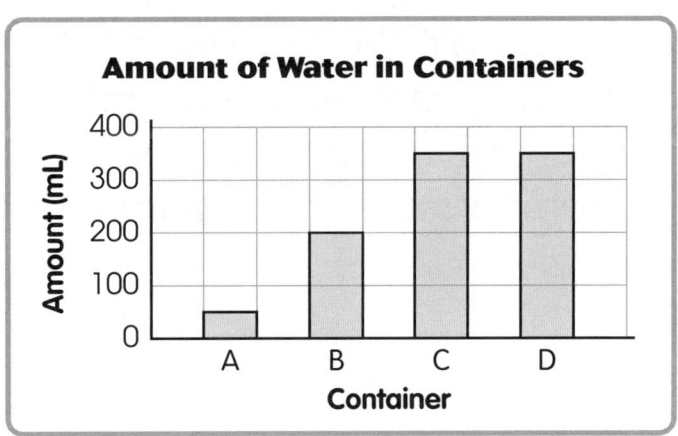

Topics covered:

Question 8
- temperature
- data management

Question 9
- addition
- capacity
- data management

ISBN: 978-1-77149-201-0

⑩ Mike wants to make 9 rectangular pyramids using sticks. How many sticks does he need in all?

⑪ Refer to question 10. If Mike uses marshmallows for the vertices of the solids, will 40 marshmallows be enough for all of the rectangular pyramids?

⑫ The highest temperatures are recorded in a city: 10°C in January, 12°C in February, and 14°C in March. If the pattern continues, what will the temperature be in June? Show the temperature on the thermometer.

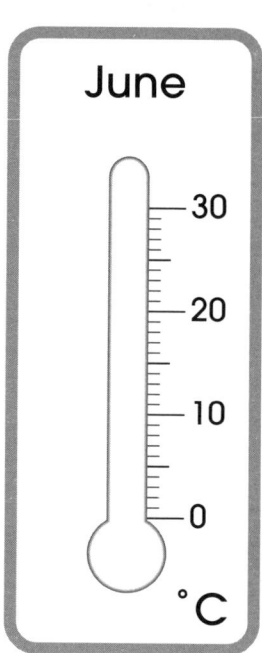

June

30

20

10

0

°C

Topics covered:

Question 10	**Question 11**	**Question 12**
• multiplication	• multiplication	• temperature
• solids	• solids	• patterning

ISBN: 978-1-77149-201-0

⑬ One carton of juice fills 4 cups. If each cup has a capacity of 500 mL, what is the total capacity of 5 juice cartons in litres?

⑭ In a deck of 20 cards, $\frac{1}{4}$ of them are red, 0.5 are blue, and the rest are yellow. If a card is picked at random, what is the chance that it is a yellow card?

⑮ Tania baked 250 cookies. She gives 187 of them to her relatives and divides the rest evenly among 9 friends. How many cookies does each friend get?

Topics covered:

Question 13	**Question 14**	**Question 15**
• multiplication	• fractions	• subtraction
• capacity	• decimals	• division
	• probability	

ISBN: 978-1-77149-201-0

⑯ Audrey wants to transform the shape into the design as shown. What could the transformation be? If each square has an area of 5 cm², what is the area of the design?

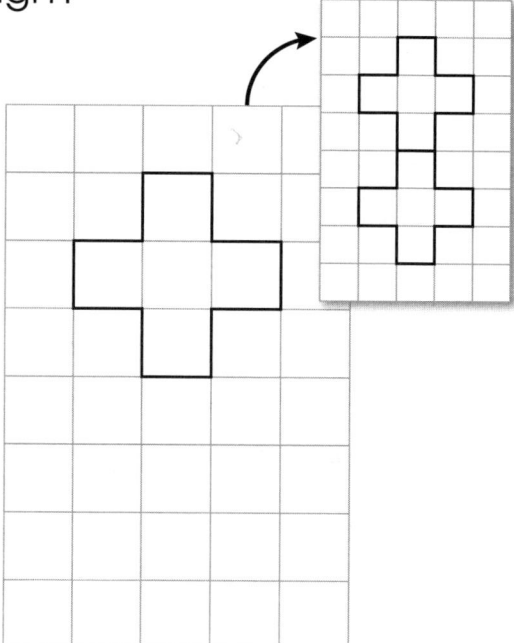

⑰ The triangles below follow a pattern starting from A1. Identify the pattern rule. Locate and draw the next 3 triangles.

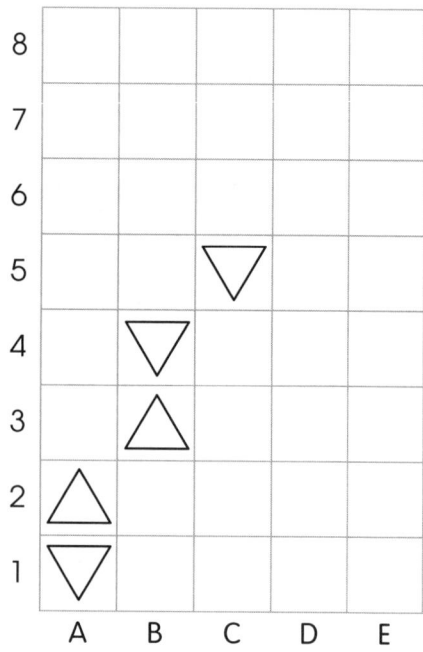

Topics covered:

Question 16
- area
- locations
- movements

Question 17
- locations
- movements
- patterning

ISBN: 978-1-77149-201-0

⑱ Caleb has 10 marbles in his bag. $\frac{4}{5}$ are red and the rest are blue. If Caleb takes away 4 red marbles and puts 4 blue marbles in the bag, what is the chance of picking a blue marble?

⑲ Greg has 4 sticks. Two of them measure 13 cm each and the other 2 measure 6 cm each. What possible shapes can Greg make using these sticks? Find the perimeter.

⑳ Jacob unfolded the rectangular prism. How many squares does the net cover on a centimetre grid paper?

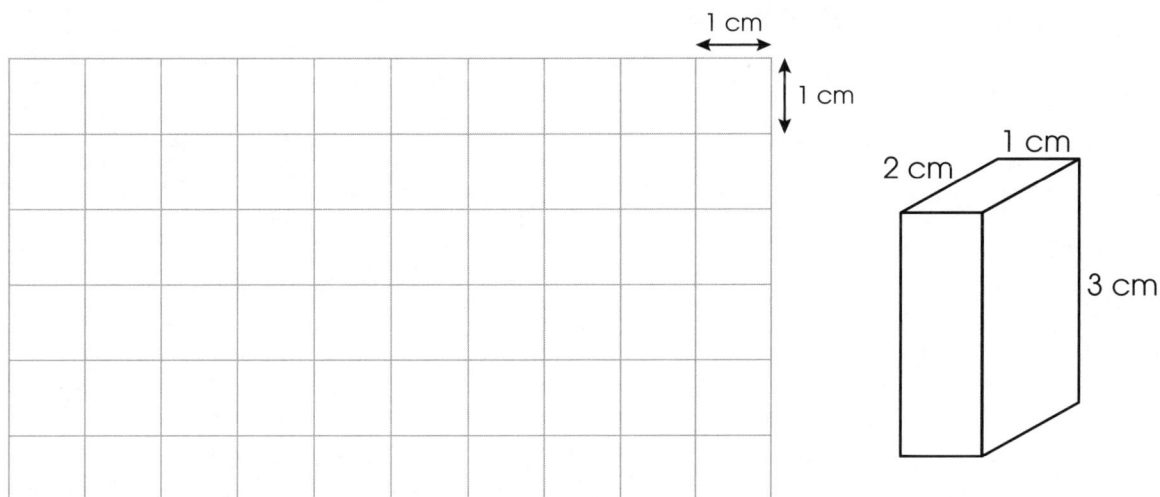

Topics covered:

Question 18	**Question 19**	**Question 20**
• fractions	• perimeter	• area
• probability	• shapes	• solids

ISBN: 978-1-77149-201-0

Students are required to solve multi-step questions which involve various topics in each.

Topics Covered

	Number Sense and Numeration	Measurement	Geometry and Spatial Sense	Patterning and Algebra	Data Management and Probability	My Record ✔ correct ✗ incorrect
1		area	locations movements			
2	addition	capacity			data management	
3	multiplication		solids			
4	multiplication division					
5		time		patterning		
6	fractions decimals	area				
7		time perimeter	shapes			
8	addition	capacity		patterning		
9	fractions decimals					
10	subtraction	mass				
11	multiplication division					
12	division fractions					
13	division	mass				
14			solids		probability	
15	money				probability	
16		mass		patterning	data management	
17		perimeter	shapes			
18	money			patterning		
19	fractions				probability	
20		perimeter	shapes			

ISBN: 978-1-77149-201-0

① Richard relocated the flower bed by translating it 2 squares down and 2 squares to the left to expand his driveway. Which squares does the new flower bed cover? What is the area of the flower bed?

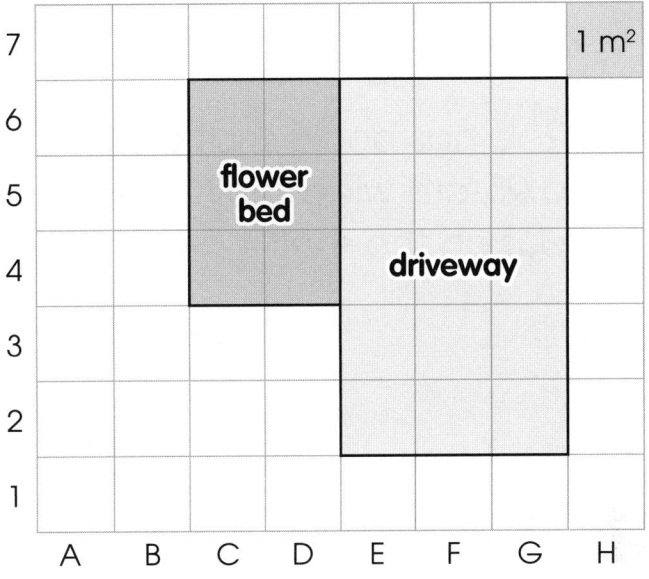

② The pictograph shows how much each container can hold. Which two containers combined can hold exactly 1 L of water?

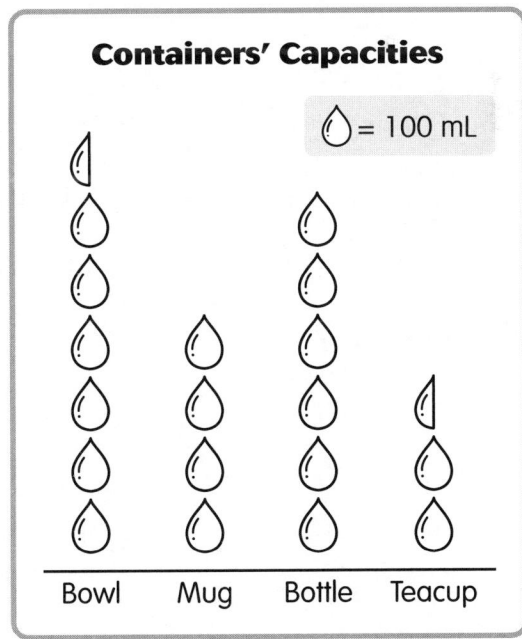

Topics covered:

Question 1
- area
- locations
- movements

Question 2
- addition
- capacity
- data management

ISBN: 978-1-77149-201-0

③ Isaac cut a stick into equal pieces to make a triangular prism. If each piece is 7 cm long, how long was the stick?

④ Rob has books that are each 5 cm thick. He puts 9 of them on a 95-cm wide shelf. How many more 5-cm thick books can he put on the shelf?

⑤ 10 people cross a bridge every 10 minutes. How many people crossed the bridge from 12:45 to 1:15?

⑥ Claire drew 10 rectangles on a wall using a stencil. She painted $\frac{3}{10}$ of them blue, 0.1 purple, and the rest green. If the area of each rectangle was 2 m², what was the area that was painted green?

Topics covered:

Question 3	Question 4	Question 5	Question 6
• multiplication	• multiplication	• time	• fractions
• solids	• division	• patterning	• decimals
			• area

ISBN: 978-1-77149-201-0

⑦ Joey's neighbourhood is in the shape of a rectangle. It takes her 15 minutes to run the length of her neighbourhood and 10 minutes to run the width. If Joey starts running at 9:30, what time will it be after she runs 2 laps around her neighbourhood?

⑧ A balloon is being filled. Sam measured the amount of water the balloon holds each second. They are 120 mL, 240 mL, and 360 mL. If the pattern continues, after how many more seconds will it reach a capacity of 720 mL?

⑨ There are 20 students in Ms. Leanne's class. 0.4 of them play hockey, $\frac{1}{5}$ of them play soccer, and the rest play volleyball. How many students play volleyball?

Topics covered:

Question 7	**Question 8**	**Question 9**
• time	• addition	• fractions
• perimeter	• capacity	• decimals
• shapes	• patterning	

ISBN: 978-1-77149-201-0

⑩ Laura's bag weighed 3 kg. She took out a book that weighs 700 g, her wallet that weighs 250 g, and her phone that weighs 130 g. Is her bag heavier or lighter than 2 kg now?

⑪ Riley has bought 3 cartons of eggs. Each carton has 6 eggs. It takes 2 eggs to make a plate of scrambled eggs. How many plates of scrambled eggs can Riley make?

⑫ Of the 20 beads Nancy has in a container, $\frac{3}{5}$ of them are red. If she divides these beads equally to make 4 identical bracelets, how many red beads will there be on each bracelet?

Topics covered:

Question 10	**Question 11**	**Question 12**
• subtraction	• multiplication	• division
• mass	• division	• fractions

ISBN: 978-1-77149-201-0

⑬ An empty crate weighed 2000 g. After filling it up with melons, it now weighs 18 kg. If each melon has a mass of 2 kg, how many melons are there in the crate?

⑭ Preston has 3 cylinders, 2 cones, and 5 spheres. One of the solids is painted. What is the chance that the painted solid can roll? What is the chance that it cannot be stacked?

⑮ Thomas had $7.85 in the fewest coins in a jar. He spent 3 quarters. If one of the remaining coins has a dent, what is the chance that it is a toonie?

Topics covered:

Question 13	**Question 14**	**Question 15**
• division	• solids	• money
• mass	• probability	• probability

⑯ Connor tracked the mass of a fruit growing in his garden. Based on the graph, how many more weeks will it be until the fruit weighs more than 1 kg?

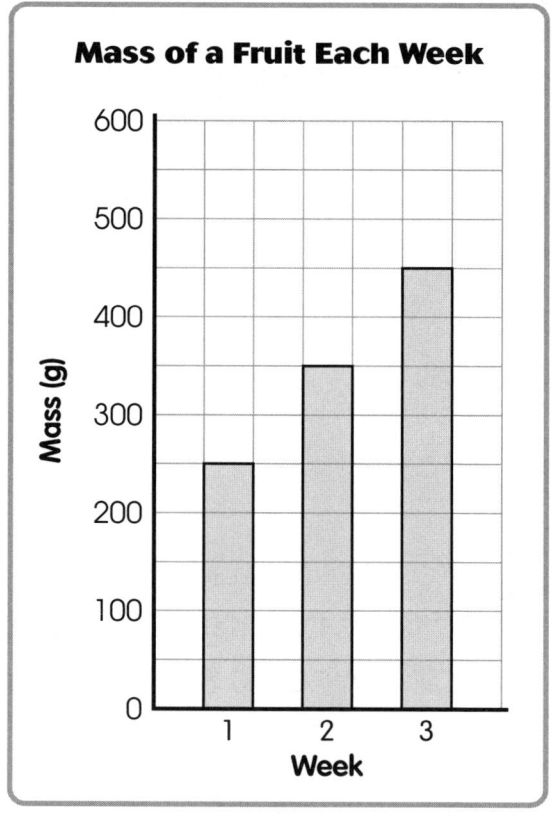

Mass of a Fruit Each Week

⑰ A square and 2 triangles with the given dimensions were combined to form a trapezoid. What is the perimeter of the trapezoid?

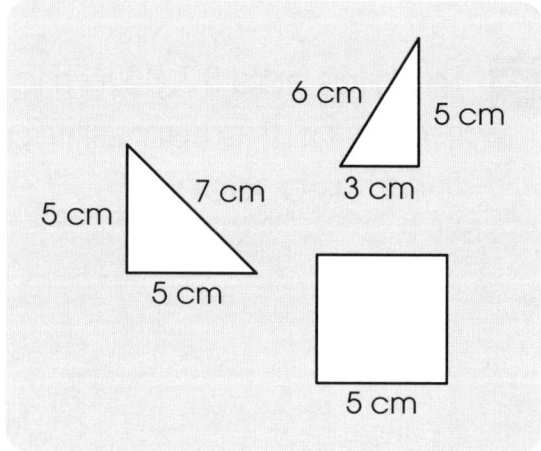

Topics covered:

Question 16
• mass
• patterning
• data management

Question 17
• perimeter
• shapes

ISBN: 978-1-77149-201-0

18 Izzy spends her allowance every day. After spending, she has $7.10 on Day 1, $6.60 on Day 2, and $6.10 on Day 3. If the pattern continues, how much will she have after spending money on Day 5?

19 A spinner has 6 equal parts and is coloured red, green, and blue. If it is equally likely that the spinner will land on red or on green, what fraction of the spinner could be blue? Write all possible fractions.

20 Jacob cuts the rectangle shown into 1 big square and 2 small squares. What is the perimeter of the big square?

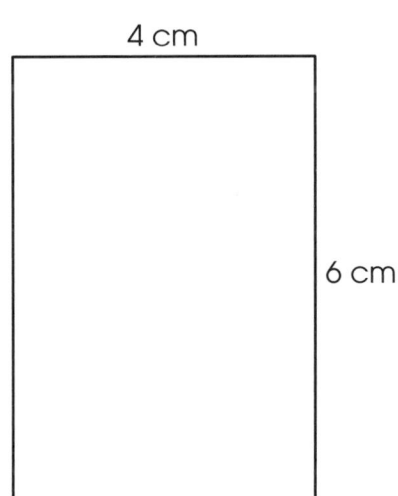

4 cm

6 cm

Topics covered:

Question 18
- money
- patterning

Question 19
- fractions
- probability

Question 20
- perimeter
- shapes

ISBN: 978-1-77149-201-0

ISBN: 978-1-77149-201-0

Answers

Basic Problem-solving Questions

1 Addition

Math Skills

1. 151
2. 512
3. 917
4. 1573
5. 1193
6. 1503
7. 1475
8. 1200
9. 165
10. 308
11. 556
12. 856
13. 1074
14. 993
15. 637
16. 1562
17. 1695
18. 1141
19a. 627 ; 607 ; 1234
   b. 607 ; 987 ; 1594 (candies)
   c. 627 ; 987 ; 1614 (candies)

Problem Solving

121 ; 121 ; 121

1. 14 + 17 = 31
   No ; will not

$$\begin{array}{r} 14 \\ + 17 \\ \hline 31 \end{array}$$

2a. 24 + 24 = 48
    48

$$\begin{array}{r} 24 \\ + 24 \\ \hline 48 \end{array}$$

b. 29 + 43 = 72
   72

$$\begin{array}{r} 29 \\ + 43 \\ \hline 72 \end{array}$$

c. Amount earned today: $129 + $58 = $187
   Total amount earned: $129 + $187 = $316

$$\begin{array}{r} 129 \\ + 58 \\ \hline 187 \end{array} \qquad \begin{array}{r} 129 \\ + 187 \\ \hline 316 \end{array}$$

316

3a. Estimate: 17 → 20
              18 → 20
              20 + 20 = 40

$$\begin{array}{r} 20 \\ + 20 \\ \hline 40 \end{array}$$

40

b. 17 + 18 = 35
   35

$$\begin{array}{r} 17 \\ + 18 \\ \hline 35 \end{array}$$

c. 35 + 35 = 70
   70

$$\begin{array}{r} 35 \\ + 35 \\ \hline 70 \end{array}$$

4. $235 + $285 = $520
   Simon does not have
   enough money.

$$\begin{array}{r} 235 \\ + 285 \\ \hline 520 \end{array}$$

5a. 54 + 54 = 108
    108 students take the bus.

$$\begin{array}{r} 54 \\ + 54 \\ \hline 108 \end{array}$$

b. 108 + 276 = 384
   384 students attend
   Meadow Ridge Public School.

$$\begin{array}{r} 108 \\ + 276 \\ \hline 384 \end{array}$$

c. 384 + 219 = 603
   603 students attend
   Westview Public School.

$$\begin{array}{r} 384 \\ + 219 \\ \hline 603 \end{array}$$

6a. 219 + 182 = 401
    Mr. Wilson needs
    401 boards in all.

$$\begin{array}{r} 219 \\ + 182 \\ \hline 401 \end{array}$$

b. 1892 + 591 = 2483
   No, one box of 2400 nails
   is not enough.

$$\begin{array}{r} 1892 \\ + 591 \\ \hline 2483 \end{array}$$

7a. 719 + 517 = 1236
    1236 pairs of shoes
    were sold.

$$\begin{array}{r} 719 \\ + 517 \\ \hline 1236 \end{array}$$

b. Sneakers sold in Greenville: 719 + 386 = 1105
   Total sold in Greenville: 175 + 1105 = 1280

$$\begin{array}{r} 719 \\ + 386 \\ \hline 1105 \end{array} \qquad \begin{array}{r} 175 \\ + 1105 \\ \hline 1280 \end{array}$$

The store in Greenville sold more shoes.

8. 316 + 316 = 632
   632 passengers arrived
   at the airport.

$$\begin{array}{r} 316 \\ + 316 \\ \hline 632 \end{array}$$

9. 288 + 288 + 288 = 864
   Fluffy will eat 864 cat treats
   in 3 weeks.

$$\begin{array}{r} 288 \\ 288 \\ + 288 \\ \hline 864 \end{array}$$

10a. $929 + $587 = $1516
     The two team raised
     $1516 altogether.

$$\begin{array}{r} 929 \\ + 587 \\ \hline 1516 \end{array}$$

b. Team D: $587 + $335 = $922
   Team C and D: $813 + $922 = $1735

$$\begin{array}{r} 587 \\ + 335 \\ \hline 922 \end{array} \qquad \begin{array}{r} 813 \\ + 922 \\ \hline 1735 \end{array}$$

Yes, Team C and Team D raised more money.

c. $1516 + $1735 = $3251
   Yes, the scouts were able
   to raise enough money.

$$\begin{array}{r} 1516 \\ + 1735 \\ \hline 3251 \end{array}$$

11a. 1375 + 1084 = 2459
     Mike needs to bike
     2459 m.

$$\begin{array}{r} 1375 \\ + 1084 \\ \hline 2459 \end{array}$$

b. 975 + 1150 = 2125
   Yes, this route is shorter than
   Mike's current route.

$$\begin{array}{r} 975 \\ + 1150 \\ \hline 2125 \end{array}$$

12a. 5038 + 4766 = 9804
     9804 people watched
     "Steelman" in the first
     two weeks.

$$\begin{array}{r} 5038 \\ + 4766 \\ \hline 9804 \end{array}$$

b. 5038 + 5266 = 10 304
   10 304 people watched
   one of the movies during
   Week 1.

$$\begin{array}{r} 5038 \\ + 5266 \\ \hline 10304 \end{array}$$

c. "Outside In": 5266 + 3441 = 8707

$$\begin{array}{r} 5266 \\ + 3441 \\ \hline 8707 \end{array}$$

"Steelman" was more popular because more people watched it.

ISBN: 978-1-77149-201-0

■··**Answers** ··

2 Subtraction

Math Skills

1. 56	2. 68	3. 48
4. 284	5. 579	6. 869
7. 67	8. 217	9. 6
10. 29	11. 488	12. 399
13. 148	14. 322	15. 142
16. 88	17. 754	18. 379

19a. 816 ; 462 ; 354
  b. 816 ; 543 ; 273

Problem Solving

33 ; 33 ; 33

1. $47 - 28 = 19$
   19

$$\begin{array}{r} 47 \\ -\ 28 \\ \hline 19 \end{array}$$

2a. $60 - 32 = 28$
   28

$$\begin{array}{r} 60 \\ -\ 32 \\ \hline 28 \end{array}$$

  b. $28 - 19 = 9$
   9

$$\begin{array}{r} 28 \\ -\ 19 \\ \hline 9 \end{array}$$

3. $94 - 79 = 15$
   15

$$\begin{array}{r} 94 \\ -\ 79 \\ \hline 15 \end{array}$$

4. $75 - 55 = 20$
   20

$$\begin{array}{r} 75 \\ -\ 55 \\ \hline 20 \end{array}$$

5a. Estimate: $51 \longrightarrow 50$
            $39 \longrightarrow 40$
   $\$50 - \$40 = \$10$
   will

$$\begin{array}{r} 50 \\ -\ 40 \\ \hline 10 \end{array}$$

  b. $\$51 - \$39 = \$12$
   12

$$\begin{array}{r} 51 \\ -\ 39 \\ \hline 12 \end{array}$$

6. $100 - 27 = 73$
   Sam's last test score
   was 73.

$$\begin{array}{r} 100 \\ -\ 27 \\ \hline 73 \end{array}$$

7. $200 - 86 = 114$
   Lucy needs to collect
   114 more pop tabs.

$$\begin{array}{r} 200 \\ -\ 86 \\ \hline 114 \end{array}$$

8. $216 - 87 = 129$
   129 students were in
   the audience.

$$\begin{array}{r} 216 \\ -\ 87 \\ \hline 129 \end{array}$$

9. $331 - 74 = 257$
   Louis needs to read
   257 more pages.

$$\begin{array}{r} 331 \\ -\ 74 \\ \hline 257 \end{array}$$

10a. $311 - 122 = 189$
   There were 189 people
   there yesterday.

$$\begin{array}{r} 311 \\ -\ 122 \\ \hline 189 \end{array}$$

  b. $189 - 102 = 87$
   87 people were not at
   the library.

$$\begin{array}{r} 189 \\ -\ 102 \\ \hline 87 \end{array}$$

11a. $2000 - 451 = 1549$
   1549 pieces are not
   put together.

$$\begin{array}{r} 2000 \\ -\ 451 \\ \hline 1549 \end{array}$$

  b. $1549 - 89 = 1460$
   1460 of them do not
   have straight edges.

$$\begin{array}{r} 1549 \\ -\ 89 \\ \hline 1460 \end{array}$$

12a. $278 - 196 = 82$
   The hill is 82 cm taller.

$$\begin{array}{r} 278 \\ -\ 196 \\ \hline 82 \end{array}$$

  b. $196 - 167 = 29$
   The house is 29 cm tall.

$$\begin{array}{r} 196 \\ -\ 167 \\ \hline 29 \end{array}$$

13a. $800 - 546 = 254$
   254 more words are needed.

$$\begin{array}{r} 800 \\ -\ 546 \\ \hline 254 \end{array}$$

  b. $964 - 800 = 164$
   Anita's story has
   164 extra words.

$$\begin{array}{r} 964 \\ -\ 800 \\ \hline 164 \end{array}$$

  c. $964 - 96 = 868$
   Anita's story has 868 words
   now.

$$\begin{array}{r} 964 \\ -\ 96 \\ \hline 868 \end{array}$$

14. $2142 - 1486 - 156 = 500$
   500 roses are left.

$$\begin{array}{r} 2142 \\ -\ 1486 \\ \hline 656 \\ -\ 156 \\ \hline 500 \end{array}$$

15. $3600 - 2498 = 1102$
   The cruise ship can carry
   1102 more passengers.

$$\begin{array}{r} 3600 \\ -\ 2498 \\ \hline 1102 \end{array}$$

16a. $5992 - 4776 = 1216$
   There were 1216 more
   male athletes.

$$\begin{array}{r} 5992 \\ -\ 4776 \\ \hline 1216 \end{array}$$

  b. $4776 - 4329 = 447$
   There were 447 more
   female athletes.

$$\begin{array}{r} 4776 \\ -\ 4329 \\ \hline 447 \end{array}$$

  c. $6296 - 5992 = 304$
   There were 304 fewer
   male athletes.

$$\begin{array}{r} 6296 \\ -\ 5992 \\ \hline 304 \end{array}$$

3 Multiplication

Math Skills

1. 6	2. 8	3. 15	4. 16
5. 32	6. 35	7. 6	8. 45
9. 28	10. 50	11. 10	12. 42
13. 18	14. 10	15. 27	16. 24
17. 36	18. 16	19. 30	20. 90
21. 48	22. 49	23. 21	24. 54
25. 18	26. 24	27. 40	28. 70
29. 63			

ISBN: 978-1-77149-201-0

Problem Solving

12 ; 12 ; 12

1. $5 \times 3 = 15$

    15

    $\begin{array}{r} 5 \\ \times\ 3 \\ \hline 15 \end{array}$

2a. $3 \times 7 = 21$

    21

    $\begin{array}{r} 3 \\ \times\ 7 \\ \hline 21 \end{array}$

  b. $2 \times 6 = 12$

    12

    $\begin{array}{r} 2 \\ \times\ 6 \\ \hline 12 \end{array}$

3. $9 \times 5 = 45$

    45

    $\begin{array}{r} 9 \\ \times\ 5 \\ \hline 45 \end{array}$

4a. $4 \times 6 = 24$

    24

    $\begin{array}{r} 4 \\ \times\ 6 \\ \hline 24 \end{array}$

  b. $7 \times 3 = 21$

    Isaac

    $\begin{array}{r} 7 \\ \times\ 3 \\ \hline 21 \end{array}$

5. $8 \times 3 = 24$

    will not

    $\begin{array}{r} 8 \\ \times\ 3 \\ \hline 24 \end{array}$

6a. $2 \times 7 = 14$

    14 scoops of ice cream
    were sold as cones.

    $\begin{array}{r} 2 \\ \times\ 7 \\ \hline 14 \end{array}$

  b. $3 \times 4 = 12$

    12 scoops of ice cream
    were sold as sundaes.

    $\begin{array}{r} 3 \\ \times\ 4 \\ \hline 12 \end{array}$

  c. $\$5 \times 7 = \$35$

    Mike made $35 by selling cones.

    $\begin{array}{r} 5 \\ \times\ 7 \\ \hline 35 \end{array}$

  d. $\$7 \times 4 = \$28$

    Mike made $28 by selling
    sundaes.

    $\begin{array}{r} 7 \\ \times\ 4 \\ \hline 28 \end{array}$

7. $6 \times 9 = 54$

    There are 54 bananas.

    $\begin{array}{r} 6 \\ \times\ 9 \\ \hline 54 \end{array}$

8. $8 \times 6 = 48$

    Karla needs 48 beads in all.

    $\begin{array}{r} 8 \\ \times\ 6 \\ \hline 48 \end{array}$

9a. $2 \times 3 = 6$

    There are 6 cucumber plants.

    $\begin{array}{r} 2 \\ \times\ 3 \\ \hline 6 \end{array}$

  b. $6 \times 6 = 36$

    Farmer Ben has 36 cucumbers.

    $\begin{array}{r} 6 \\ \times\ 6 \\ \hline 36 \end{array}$

10a. $10 \times 2 = 20$

    Bryan and his sister have
    20 crayons altogether.

    $\begin{array}{r} 10 \\ \times\ 2 \\ \hline 20 \end{array}$

  b. $10 \times 4 = 40$

    Mrs. Lane's children have
    40 crayons in all.

    $\begin{array}{r} 10 \\ \times\ 4 \\ \hline 40 \end{array}$

11. $10 \times 6 = 60$

    There are 60 players in
    the league.

    $\begin{array}{r} 10 \\ \times\ 6 \\ \hline 60 \end{array}$

12a. $3 \times 5 = 15$

    15 cookies were eaten.

    $\begin{array}{r} 3 \\ \times\ 5 \\ \hline 15 \end{array}$

  b. Total cookies: $10 \times 3 = 30$

    Cookies eaten in 7 days: $4 \times 7 = 28$

    $\begin{array}{r} 10 \\ \times\ 3 \\ \hline 30 \end{array}$ $\qquad$ $\begin{array}{r} 4 \\ \times\ 7 \\ \hline 28 \end{array}$

    Patrick would not have finished all the
    cookies.

13. $2 + 3 = 5$

    $5 \times 7 = 35$

    Hannah will learn 35 new words.

    $\begin{array}{r} 5 \\ \times\ 7 \\ \hline 35 \end{array}$

14a. "Twice" means 2 times.

    $2 \times 2 = 4$

    Naomi will have 4 hours
    of practice in 1 week.

    $\begin{array}{r} 2 \\ \times\ 2 \\ \hline 4 \end{array}$

  b. $4 \times 5 = 20$

    Naomi will have 20 hours
    of practice in 5 weeks.

    $\begin{array}{r} 4 \\ \times\ 5 \\ \hline 20 \end{array}$

15a. Cost each day: $\$3 \times 2 = \$6$

    Spending in 5 days: $\$6 \times 5 = \$30$

    $\begin{array}{r} 3 \\ \times\ 2 \\ \hline 6 \end{array}$ $\qquad$ $\begin{array}{r} 6 \\ \times\ 5 \\ \hline 30 \end{array}$

    Ms. Carol will spend $30 in 5 days.

  b. $\$5 \times 5 = \$25$

    Ms. Carol has to pay $25 instead.

    $\begin{array}{r} 5 \\ \times\ 5 \\ \hline 25 \end{array}$

4 Division

Math Skills

1.

    2

2.

    3

3.

    2

4.

    3

5. $\begin{array}{r} 4 \\ 4\overline{)16} \\ \underline{16} \\ \end{array}$

6. $\begin{array}{r} 9\,R\,1 \\ 5\overline{)46} \\ \underline{45} \\ 1 \end{array}$

ISBN: 978-1-77149-201-0

7.
$$3\overline{)27}$$ = 9
27

8.
$$2\overline{)11}$$ = 5R1
10
1

9.
$$6\overline{)24}$$ = 4
24

10.
$$7\overline{)22}$$ = 3R1
21
1

11. 7
12. 4
13. 7R1
14. 6
15. 8
16. 9R1
17. 8R4
18. 9R1
19. 7

Problem Solving

2 ; 2

1.

15 ÷ 5 = 3
3

2. 30 ÷ 6 = 5
5

$$6\overline{)30}$$ = 5
30

3. 64 ÷ 8 = 8
8

$$8\overline{)64}$$ = 8
64

4. 56 ÷ 8 = 7
7

$$8\overline{)56}$$ = 7
56

5a. There are 3 people.
12 ÷ 3 = 4
4

$$3\overline{)12}$$ = 4
12

b. There are 4 people.
12 ÷ 4 = 3
3

$$4\overline{)12}$$ = 3
12

6. 49 ÷ 7 = 7
will

$$7\overline{)49}$$ = 7
49

7. 60 ÷ 6 = 10
Melody will write 10 holiday
cards in an hour.

$$6\overline{)60}$$ = 10
60

8. Buns eaten each day: 2 + 2 = 4
Days to finish 12 buns: 12 ÷ 4 = 3
They will finish 12 buns in 3 days.

$$4\overline{)12}$$ = 3
12

9a. 37 ÷ 5 = 7R2
Aunt Jenny can sew
buttons onto 7 shirts.
b. 2 buttons remain.

$$5\overline{)37}$$ = 7R2
35
2

10. 26 ÷ 6 = 4R2
5 tables are needed to
seat all of the guests.

$$6\overline{)26}$$ = 4R2
24
2

11. 34 ÷ 8 = 4R2
2 muffins cannot be
packaged.

$$8\overline{)34}$$ = 4R2
32
2

12a. There are 7 people.
24 ÷ 7 = 3R3
Each person gets 3 bottles
of water. 3 bottles remain.

$$7\overline{)24}$$ = 3R3
21
3

b. There are 8 people.
24 ÷ 8 = 3
Yes, all the bottles of water
can be divided equally.

$$8\overline{)24}$$ = 3
24

13. 20 ÷ 3 = 6R2
Arthur can buy 6 toy cars
at most.

$$3\overline{)20}$$ = 6R2
18
2

14a. 24 ÷ 6 = 4
There are 4 shirts in each
stack.

$$6\overline{)24}$$ = 4
24

b. 24 ÷ 8 = 3
There will be 3 stacks.

$$8\overline{)24}$$ = 3
24

15a. 17 ÷ 2 = 8R1
She can buy 8 packs of
spaghetti at most.

$$2\overline{)17}$$ = 8R1
16
1

b. 45 ÷ 8 = 5R5
5 meatballs will be left.

$$8\overline{)45}$$ = 5R5
40
5

16a. 72 ÷ 9 = 8
There are 8 pages in each
chapter.

$$9\overline{)72}$$ = 8
72

b. 56 ÷ 8 = 7
Zara spends 7 minutes
reading a page.

$$8\overline{)56}$$ = 7
56

c. 64 ÷ 8 = 8
Leo spends 8 minutes
reading a page.

$$8\overline{)64}$$ = 8
64

17a. 26 ÷ 6 = 4R2
There are 4 teams of 6.

$$6\overline{)26}$$ = 4R2
24
2

b. 2 teams will have 7 students.

5 Fractions and Decimals

Math Skills

1. $\frac{3}{6}$; $\frac{5}{8}$; $\frac{3}{5}$; $\frac{3}{12}$; $\frac{5}{15}$

2.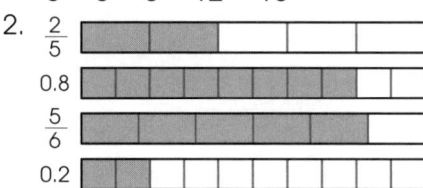

$\frac{2}{5}$

0.8

$\frac{5}{6}$

0.2

0.2 ; $\frac{2}{5}$; 0.8 ; $\frac{5}{6}$

Problem Solving

3

ISBN: 978-1-77149-201-0

1a. 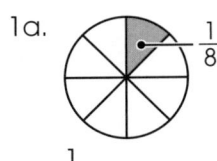 $\frac{1}{8}$

1

b. 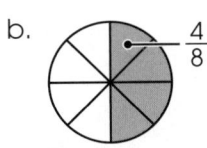 $\frac{4}{8}$

Kyle

2a. 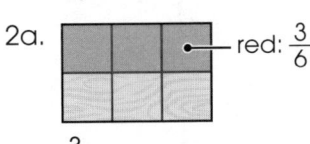 red: $\frac{3}{6}$

$\frac{3}{6}$

b. 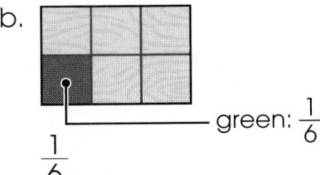 green: $\frac{1}{6}$

$\frac{1}{6}$

c. 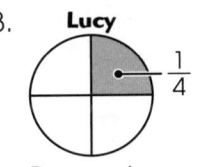 not painted: $\frac{2}{6}$

$\frac{2}{6}$

3. **Lucy** **Bernard**

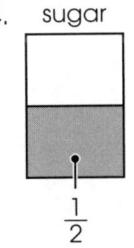 $\frac{1}{4}$ 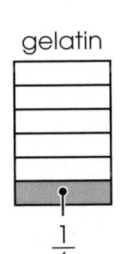 $\frac{1}{3}$

Bernard

4. sugar   gelatin

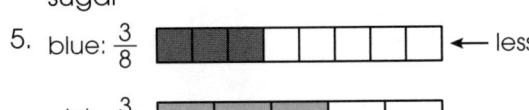

$\frac{1}{2}$ $\frac{1}{6}$

sugar

5. blue: $\frac{3}{8}$ 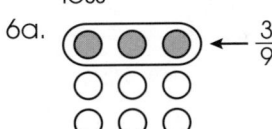 ← less

pink: $\frac{3}{5}$

less

6a. ← $\frac{3}{9}$

$\frac{3}{9}$ of Arnold's collection is red.

b. $\frac{1}{6}$ of 12 →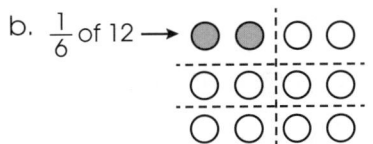

Greg has 2 red toy cars.

c. 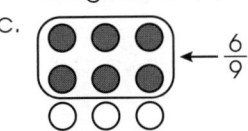 ← $\frac{6}{9}$

$\frac{6}{9}$ of Arnold's collection is blue.

d. $\frac{1}{3}$ of 12 →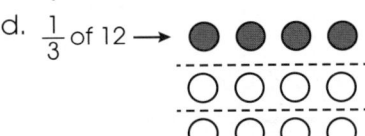

Greg has 4 blue toy cars. Arnold has more blue toy cars.

7a. 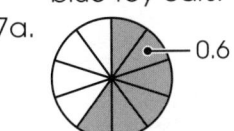 0.6

6 slices were eaten.

b. 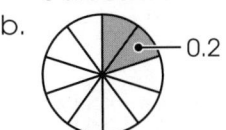 0.2

Caleb ate 0.2 of the cake.

8a.  0.2

2 slices were used.

b. 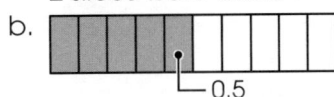 0.5

Amy used 0.5 of the loaf.

9a. wrapping: 0.5 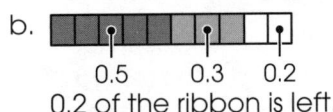 ← more

bow: 0.3

Sue used more ribbon to wrap the gift.

b.

0.5   0.3   0.2

0.2 of the ribbon is left.

10a.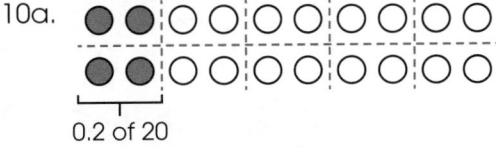

0.2 of 20

4 students wear glasses.

b.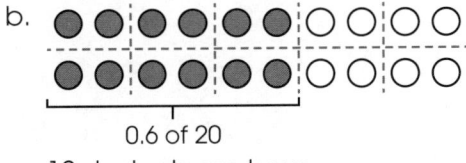

0.6 of 20

12 students are boys.

ISBN: 978-1-77149-201-0

c.

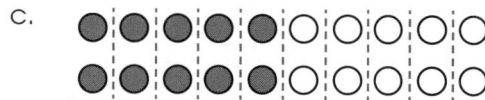

10 students = 0.5 of 20

0.5 of the class goes to school by school bus.

11a.

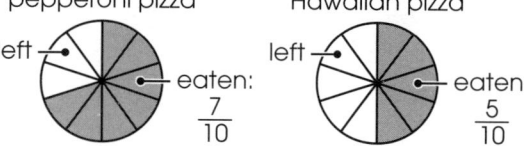

pepperoni pizza

left — eaten: $\frac{7}{10}$

Hawaiian pizza

left — eaten: $\frac{5}{10}$

5 – 3 = 2

The pepperoni pizza has fewer slices left. It has 2 fewer slices left than the Hawaiian pizza.

b. 0.7 of the pepperoni pizza was eaten.

c.

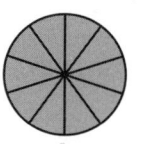 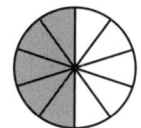

$1\frac{1}{2}$ pizza = 15 slices

Number of slices eaten: 7 + 5 = 12

No, Emily is not correct.

12a.

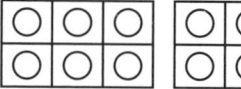 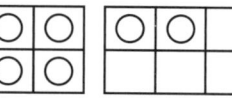

$2\frac{2}{6}$ boxes of light bulbs: 14 light bulbs

No, Mr. Richards does not have enough light bulbs.

b. Light bulbs needed: 20 – 14 = 6
6 light bulbs = 1 box
Mr. Richards needs 1 more box of light bulbs.

6 Money

Math Skills

1a. 8 ; 30 ; 8.30   b. 2 ; 80 ; 2.80
c. 30 ; 50 ; 30.50   d. 15 ; 60 ; 15.60

2. a.   b.   c.

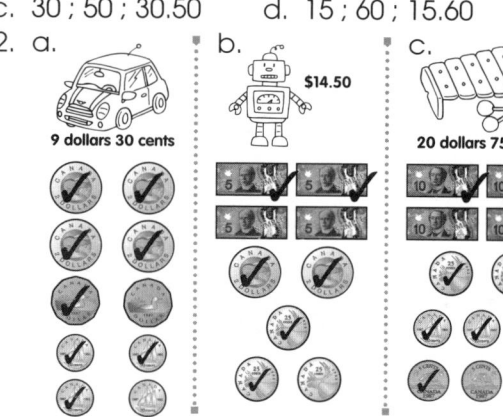

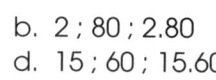

Problem Solving

12 ; 25 ; 24 ; 50 ; 24.50

1. $6.50 = 6 dollars 50 cents
$4.75 = 4 dollars 75 cents
$6.50 + $4.75 = $11.25

dollars	cents
6	50
+ 4	75
11 ~~10~~	~~125~~ 25

11.25

2a. $3.75 = 3 dollars 75 cents
$0.80 = 80 cents
$3.75 + $0.80 = $4.55

dollars	cents
3	75
+ 0	80
4 ~~3~~	~~155~~ 55

4.55

b. $3.75 = 3 dollars 75 cents
$4.55 = 4 dollars 55 cents
$3.75 + $4.55 = $8.30

dollars	cents
3	75
+ 4	55
8 ~~7~~	~~130~~ 30

8.30

c. $4.55 = 4 dollars 55 cents
$4.55 + $4.55 = $9.10

dollars	cents
4	55
+ 4	55
9 ~~8~~	~~110~~ 10

9.10

3. $3.80 = 3 dollars 80 cents
$1.75 = 1 dollar 75 cents
$3.80 – $1.75 = $2.05

dollars	cents
3	80
– 1	75
2	05

2.05

4. $8.10 = 8 dollars 10 cents
$5.85 = 5 dollars 85 cents
$8.10 – $5.85 = $2.25

dollars	cents
⁷$\cancel{8}$	~~10~~ ¹¹⁰
– 5	85
2	25

2.25

5. $4.95 = 4 dollars 95 cents
$4.70 = 4 dollars 70 cents
$4.95 – $4.70 = $0.25

dollars	cents
4	95
– 4	70
0	25

Store B ; 0.25

ISBN: 978-1-77149-201-0

6a. $3.15 = 3 dollars 15 cents
$3.15 + $3.15 = $6.30

dollars	cents
3	15
+ 3	15
6	30

2 binders will cost $6.30.

b. $10 = 10 dollars
$6.30 = 6 dollars 30 cents
$10 − $6.30 = $3.70

dollars	cents
$^9 \cancel{10}$	$\cancel{00}\,^{100}$
− 6	30
3	70

Fred's change will be $3.70.

7a. $10.70 = 10 dollars 70 cents
$2.50 = 2 dollars 50 cents
$10.70 − $2.50 = $8.20

dollars	cents
10	70
− 2	50
8	20

The box of crayons cost $8.20.

b. $11.80 = 11 dollars 80 cents
$8.20 = 8 dollars 20 cents
$8.20 + $11.80 = $20

dollars	cents
8	20
+ 11	80
$20\,\cancel{19}$	$\cancel{100}\,_{00}$

Alexa paid $20.

8a. $5.95 = 5 dollars 95 cents
$2.05 = 2 dollars 5 cents
$5.95 + $2.05 = $8

dollars	cents
5	95
+ 2	05
$_8\cancel{7}$	$\cancel{100}\,_{00}$

They cost $8 in total.

b. $6.05 = 6 dollars 5 cents
$6.05 + $6.05 = $12.10

dollars	cents
6	05
+ 6	05
12	10

The total cost is $12.10.

c. $6.05 = 6 dollars 5 cents
$5.85 = 5 dollars 85 cents
$6.05 − $5.85 = $0.20

dollars	cents
$^5\cancel{6}$	$\cancel{05}\,^{105}$
− 5	85
0	20

A fish burger costs $0.20 more.

d. $6.05 = 6 dollars 5 cents
$2.05 = 2 dollars 5 cents
$1.50 = 1 dollar 50 cents
$2 = 2 dollars
Cost: $6.05 + $2.05 + $1.50 = $9.60
After discount: $9.60 − $2 = $7.60

dollars	cents		dollars	cents
6	05		9	60
2	05		− 2	00
+ 1	50		7	60
9	60			

They cost $7.60 in total.

9. $5 = 5 dollars
$2.10 = 2 dollars 10 cents
$5 − $2.10 = $2.90

dollars	cents
$^4\cancel{5}$	$\cancel{00}\,^{100}$
− 2	10
2	90

Karl's change was $2.90.

10. Esther paid: ($2)($2) = $4
$4 = 4 dollars
$0.55 = 55 cents
$4 − $0.55 = $3.45

dollars	cents
$^3\cancel{4}$	$\cancel{00}\,^{100}$
− 0	55
3	45

The box of pencils cost $3.45.

11. Jim's change: ($2)(10¢)(5¢) = $2.15
$7.85 = 7 dollars 85 cents
$2.15 = 2 dollars 15 cents
$7.85 + $2.15 = $10

dollars	cents
7	85
+ 2	15
$_{10}\cancel{9}$	$\cancel{100}\,_{00}$

Jim paid $10.

12a. Amy's money: ($2)($1)(25¢) = $3.25
$4.50 = 4 dollars 50 cents
$3.25 = 3 dollars 25 cents
$4.50 − $3.25 = $1.25

dollars	cents
4	50
− 3	25
1	25

Amy needs $1.25 more.

b. Sister's money: ($2) = $2
$2 = 2 dollars
Amy's money: $3.25 + $2 = $5.25
Money left: $5.25 − $4.50 = $0.75

dollars	cents		dollars	cents
3	25		$^4\cancel{5}$	$\cancel{25}\,^{125}$
+ 2	00		− 4	50
5	25		0	75

Yes, Amy has enough to buy the doll now.
She will have $0.75 left.

13a. $2.60 = 2 dollars 60 cents
$2.60 + $2.60 = $5.20

dollars	cents
2	60
+ 2	60
$_5\cancel{4}$	$\cancel{120}\,_{20}$

Joshua spent $5.20.

ISBN: 978-1-77149-201-0

b. $10 = 10 dollars
$5.20 = 5 dollars 20 cents
$10 − $5.20 = $4.80

	dollars	cents
	⁹1̶0̶	0̶0̶ ¹⁰⁰
−	5	20
	4	80

No, Joshua did not get the correct amount of change. It should be $4.80.

c. Joshua's change should be 2 toonies, 3 quarters, and 1 nickel.

14a. Diane's change: ($2) ($2) (10¢) (10¢) = $4.20
$10 = 10 dollars
$4.20 = 4 dollars 20 cents
$2.90 = 2 dollars 90 cents
Amount spent: $10 − $4.20 = $5.80
Cost of 2 boxes: $2.90 + $2.90 = $5.80

	dollars	cents
	⁹1̶0̶	0̶0̶ ¹⁰⁰
−	4	20
	5	80

	dollars	cents
	2	90
+	2	90
	₅4̶	1̶8̶0̶ ₈₀

Diane bought 2 boxes.

b. $2.90 = 2 dollars 90 cents
$2.90 + $2.90 + $2.90 = $8.70
$10 − $8.70 = $1.30

	dollars	cents
	2	90
	2	90
+	2	90
	₈8̶	2̶7̶0̶ ₇₀

	dollars	cents
	⁹1̶0̶	0̶0̶ ¹⁰⁰
−	8	70
	1	30

Diane's change will be 1 loonie, 1 quarter, and 1 nickel.

7 Time and Temperature

Math Skills

1. A: 1 ; 55 ; 5 ; 2
B: 8:45 ; 15 minutes before 9
C: 9:15 ; 15 minutes after 9
D: 4:25 ; 25 minutes after 4

2. A: 6   B: 47°C   C: 23°C

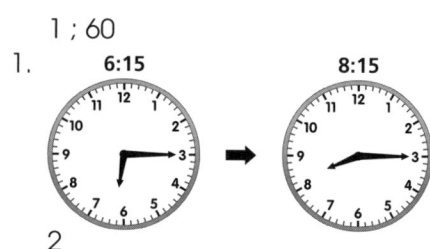

Problem Solving

1 ; 60

1.

2

2a. 7:30 → 8:10
40

b. 8:10 → 8:35
25

3. 11:45 → 1:15
1 ; 30

4a.
February 2017						
Sun	Mon	Tue	Wed	Thu	Fri	Sat
			1	2 🐭	3	4
5	6	7	8	9	10	11
12	13	14 ♡	15	16	17	18
19	20 🏠	21	22	23	24	25
26	27	28				

b. Nancy's birthday is February 4.
c. 1 week = 7 days
The test is on February 21.
d. The trip is 5 days long.

5a. A: 3   B: 24°C   C: 18°C
B ; A ; C
b. The kitchen had the highest temperature.
c. The backyard had the lowest temperature.
d. 11 − 3 = 8
The temperature rose by 8°C.
e. 11 − 8 = 3

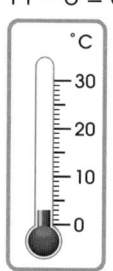

The temperature was 3°C in the evening.

6a. Susan:
Susan's body temperature is 38°C.
Susan has a fever.

ISBN: 978-1-77149-201-0

Caleb:
Caleb's body temperature is 40°C.
Caleb has a fever.
Amanda:
Amanda's body temperature is 37°C.
Amanda does not have a fever.

b. Caleb needs to see a doctor.

7a. The pot of water was cooling down because its temperature was dropping over time.

b. The temperature was dropping and was getting close to room temperature. The pot was on a table.

c. 37°C at 10:17
   30°C at 10:25

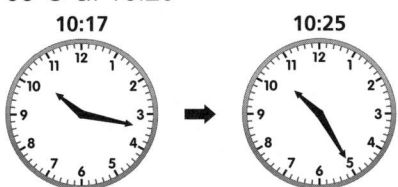

It took 8 minutes.

d. 47°C at 10:06
   23°C at 10:34

It took 28 minutes.

e. 10:11 is between 10:06 and 10:17, so the temperature should be between 37°C and 47°C.
   (Suggested answer)
   The temperature might be about 42°C.

8. 11 ; 27°C ; 18°C ; 9°C

a. "Noon" means 12:00 p.m.
   12:00 p.m.: 27°C
   5:45 p.m.: 18°C
   Change: 27 − 18 = 9
   The temperature dropped by 9°C.

b.

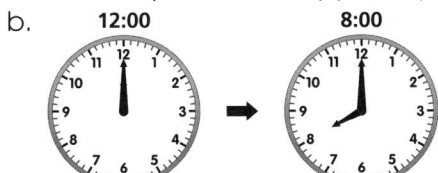

It took 8 hours.

c. From 9:00 a.m. to 12:00 p.m.: 27 − 11 = 16
   From 12:00 p.m. to 5:45 p.m.: 27 − 18 = 9
   From 5:45 p.m. to 8:00 p.m.: 18 − 9 = 9
   It was between 9:00 a.m. and 12:00 p.m.
   It took 3 hours.

d.

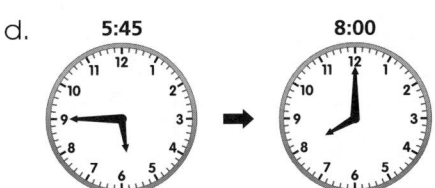

Elapsed time: 2 hours 15 minutes
Jacob was referring to the time period between 5:45 p.m. and 8:00 p.m.

e. "Noon" means 12:00 p.m.
   From 12:00 p.m. to 8:00 p.m.:
   27 − 9 = 18

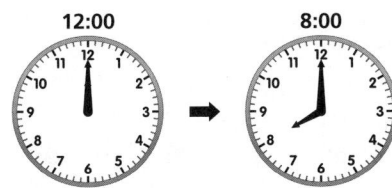

The temperature dropped by 18°C. It took 8 hours.

8 Capacity and Mass

Math Skills

1a. mL   b. L   c. mL
 d. L   e. mL
 2. A: 2 L   B: 10 L   C: 250 mL
    D: 700 mL

3a. g   b. kg   c. g
 d. kg   e. g
 4. A: 6 kg B: 1 kg   C: 4 g
    D: 230 g

Problem Solving

Janice
1. Sink A: 1580 mL
   Sink B: 1 L = 1000 mL
   A

2. Red pail: 4 L = 4000 mL
   Green pail: 3000 mL
   green

3a. 2 + 2 = 4
    4

b. 2 + 2 + 2 = 6
   6 L = 6000 mL
   6000

c. 1 jug: 2 L
   Half jug: 1 L = 1000 mL
   1000

d. Water in jug: 500 mL
   Capacity of bottle: 1 L = 1000 mL
   will not

4a.

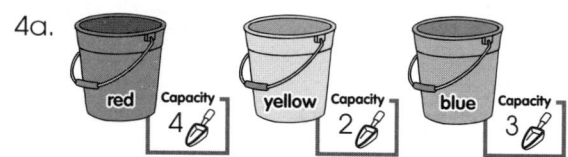

b. 2

c. 3 L = 3000 mL
3000

d. 4 + 2 + 3 = 9
9

5. Baby Theo: 3 kg = 3000 g
Baby Tina: 2850 g
Baby Theo is heavier.

6. Toy train: 1974 g
Toy truck: 2 kg = 2000 g
The toy train is lighter.

7. Dessert A: 2 kg = 2000 g ⟵ lighter
Dessert B: 3300 g
The weight of the cake was 2000 g.

8. 1 pineapple: 3 kg
2 pineapples: 6 kg = 6000 g ⟵ heavier
1 squash: 5000 g
Two pineapples weigh more than
one squash.

9a. 1 watermelon: 9 kg
3 honeydews: 9 kg
1 honeydew: 3 kg = 3000 g
The weight of 1 honeydew is 3000 g.

b. 1 papaya: 500 g
2 papayas: 1000 g = 1 kg
1 cantaloupe = 2 papayas = 1 kg
The weight of 1 cantaloupe is 1 kg.

c. 1 honeydew: 3 kg   1 cantaloupe: 1 kg
3 cantaloupes: 3 kg = 1 honeydew
3 cantaloupes are needed to balance
1 honeydew.

d. 1 papaya: 500 g   6 papayas: 3000 g
1 honeydew: 3000 g = 6 papayas
6 papayas are needed to balance
1 honeydew.

10a. 1 carton: 2 L   1 bottle: 1 L
2 bottles: 2 L
A carton of juice can fill 2 bottles.

b. 1 bottle: 4 cups   2 bottles: 8 cups
1 carton = 2 bottles = 8 cups
A carton of juice can fill 8 cups.

c. Empty bottle: 58 g   Empty cup: 90 g
90 − 58 = 32
The cup is 32 g heavier
than the bottle.

$$\begin{array}{r} 90 \\ -\ 58 \\ \hline 32 \end{array}$$

11a. Mike's thinking is not correct. A bucket
that is heavier does not mean that it has
a greater capacity.

b. Full red bucket: 10 L
Half full red bucket: 5 L
There is 5 L of water in the bucket.

12a. Cooking Pan A: 1 kg = 1000 g
Cooking Pan B: 800 g ⟵ lighter
Mr. Noah bought Cooking Pan B.

b. Cooking Pan A: 750 mL
Cooking Pan B: 1 L = 1000 mL ⟵ greater
Ms. Lee bought Cooking Pan B.

c. Cooking Pan A: 1 kg = 1000 g
Cooking Pan B: 800 g
Total weight: 1000 + 800 = 1800
The total weight of the shipment is 1800 g.

$$\begin{array}{r} 1000 \\ +\ 800 \\ \hline 1800 \end{array}$$

13a. 1 jug: 2 L
2 jugs: 4 L = 4000 mL
The capacity of 2 jugs is 4000 mL.

b. 1 jug: 1 kg
3 jugs: 3 kg = 3000 g
The weight of 3 jugs is 3000 g.

9   Perimeter and Area

Math Skills

1. Perimeter: 14 ; 10 cm ; 18 cm
Area: 10 ; 5 cm² ; 14 cm²

2. 3 ; 8 ; 6 ; 9 ; 26

3. 3 + 3 + 2 + 2 + 5 + 5 ; 20 (cm)

4. 4 + 7 + 3 + 3 + 5 ; 22 (cm)

5. 3 + 1 + 1 + 1 + 2 + 3 ; 11 (cm)

Problem Solving

30 ; 30

1. 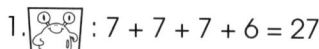 : 7 + 7 + 7 + 6 = 27

 : 3 + 2 + 4 + 2 + 3 + 7 = 21

27 ; 21

2a. 2 + 2 + 3 = 7
7

b. 4 + 3 + 4 + 3 = 14
14

c. 3 + 2 + 2 + 2 = 9
9

d. 2 + 2 + 3 + 2 + 2 + 2 = 13
13

3.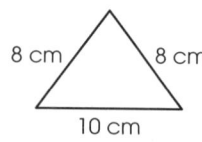

10 + 8 + 8 = 26
26

ISBN: 978-1-77149-201-0

4.

30 cm
20 cm 20 cm
30 cm

$30 + 30 + 20 + 20 = 100$
100

5.

10 m
10 m 10 m
10 m

$10 + 10 + 10 + 10 = 40$
40

6a. 8 ; 11 cm² ; 13 cm² ; 12 cm² ; 6 cm² ;
15 cm² ; 5 cm²
b. The area of the largest piece is 15 cm².
c. The area of the smallest piece is 5 cm².
d. The area of the puzzle is 70 cm².

7a. Mr. Smith ; Mr. Lee
b. Area of Mr. Smith's flower garden: 6 m²
Area of Mr. Lee's flower garden: 5 m²
Difference: $6 - 5 = 1$
Mr. Smith's flower garden covers a greater
area by 1 m² more.
c. Area of Mr. Smith's driveway: 9 m²
Area of Mr. Lee's driveway: 12 m²
Difference: $12 - 9 = 3$
Mr. Smith's driveway covers less area by
3 m².

8a. The area of the flower bed is 28 m².
b. Mr. Lee needs 58 m of fencing.
c. Perimeter of patio: $2 + 4 + 2 + 4 = 12$
Area of patio: 8
The perimeter of the patio is 12 m and the
area of the patio is 8 m².
d.

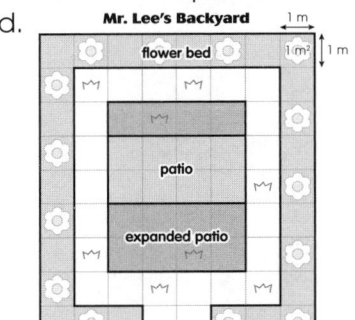

Expanded perimeter: $5 + 4 + 5 + 4 = 18$
Expanded area: 20
After the expansion, the perimeter is 18 m
and the area is 20 m².
e. Area before expansion: 36
Area after expansion: 24
Difference: $36 - 24 = 12$
The area of the lawn will decrease by
12 m² after the expansion.

9a. Perimeter: $8 + 1 + 8 + 1 = 18$
Area: 8
The perimeter is 18 cm and the area is
8 cm².
b. (Suggested drawing)

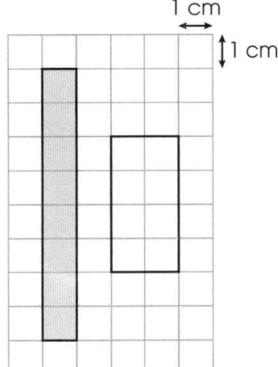

Perimeter: $4 + 2 + 4 + 2 = 12$
Its perimeter is 12 cm.

10a. Half of 6 is 3.
The width of Eric's bedroom is 3 m.
b. Perimeter: $6 + 3 + 6 + 3 = 18$
The perimeter of Eric's bedroom is 18 m.
c.

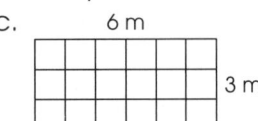

The area of Eric's bedroom is 18 m².

10 Shapes and Solids

Math Skills

Shapes:
A: rhombus   B: trapezoid
C: parallelogram   D: triangle
E: kite
Solids:
V: rectangular pyramid
W: triangular prism
X: sphere
Y: cylinder
Z: rectangular prism

Problem Solving

1.
triangle

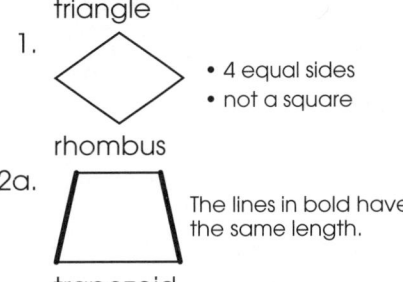

• 4 equal sides
• not a square

rhombus

2a.

The lines in bold have
the same length.

trapezoid

ISBN: 978-1-77149-201-0

b.

square   rhombus

• 4 lines of symmetry   • 2 lines of symmetry

more

c. (Suggested answer)

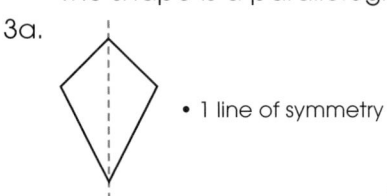

• no line of symmetry

The shape is a parallelogram.

3a.

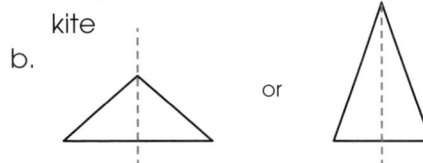

• 1 line of symmetry

kite

b.

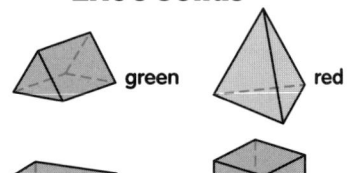

or

Both triangles have 1 line of symmetry.

triangle ; 1

c.

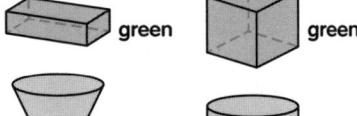

pentagon ; 5

4a. **Eric's Solids**

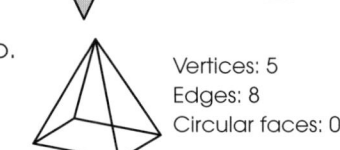

green   red

green   green

blue   blue

b.

Vertices: 5
Edges: 8
Circular faces: 0

The solid should be coloured green.

c. Solids that can roll:
The cone and the cylinder can roll.
Solids that can slide:
The triangular prism, rectangular prism, cone, triangular pyramid, cube, and cylinder can slide.
Solids that can be stacked:
The triangular prism, rectangular prism, cube, and cylinder can be stacked.

5a.

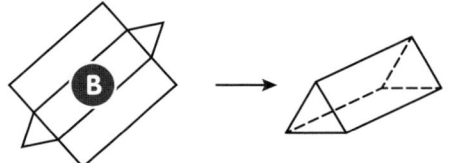

Net B folds into a triangular prism.

b.

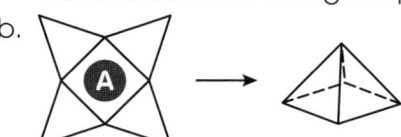

Net A folds into a square-based pyramid.

c.

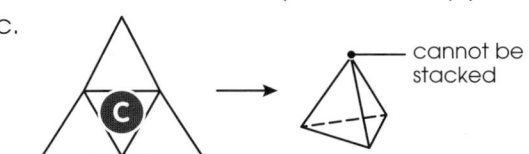

cannot be stacked

No, Net C does not fold into a solid that can be stacked.

d. Net A: 5 faces
Net B: 5 faces
Net C: 4 faces
Net C folds into a solid that has the fewest faces.

e.

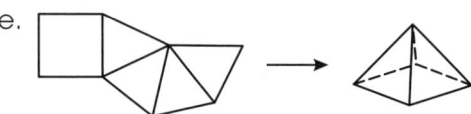

Yes, Hugo is correct.

6a. The tree:

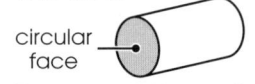

circular face

Zara used the cylinder.
The house:

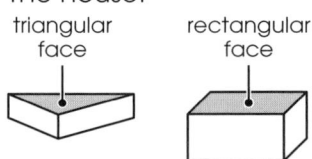

triangular face   rectangular face

Zara used the triangular prism and the rectangular prism.

b.

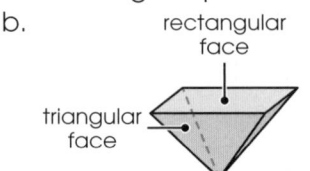

rectangular face

triangular face

Yes, it can make triangular and rectangular prints.

c. Zara can stack all the solids.
d. It was the cylinder.

ISBN: 978-1-77149-201-0

7a.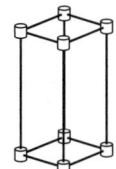

Jessie made a rectangular prism.

b.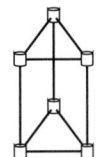

Jessie would have made a triangular prism.

8a.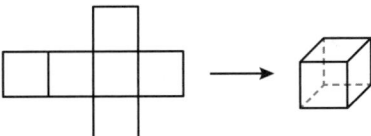

Mike makes a cube.

b.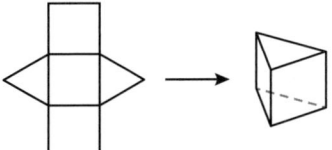

Carley makes a triangular prism.

c.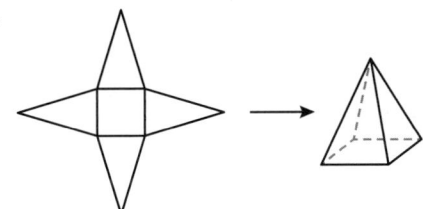

Jason's solid is a square-based pyramid.

11 Locations and Movements

Math Skills

1. Translation: B, Y   Rotation: C, X
   Reflection: A, Z

2a. B7 ; G8 ;
   F3 ; C5

b.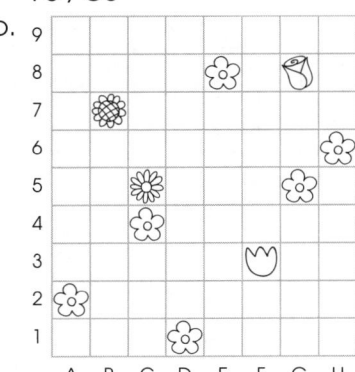

Problem Solving

   2 ; 1 ; 2 ; 1

1a. Yes ; will

b. 3 squares up ; 1 square to the right

2a. B8 ; C3

b.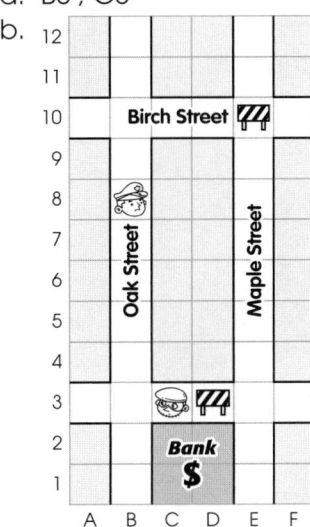

c. No ; will not

d. 5 squares down ; 1 square to the left

3a. D2 ; J5

b.

c. 3 squares up ; 6 squares to the right

d. 6 squares to the left ; 4 squares down

4a.

b. 🚀→⛽₁: The spaceship went 2 squares to the right and 2 squares up.

   ⛽₁→⛽₂: The spaceship went 3 squares down, 5 squares to the right, and 2 squares down.

c. The spaceship broke down at I3.

d. The spaceship went 2 squares up and 1 square to the right.

ISBN: 978-1-77149-201-0

5a. translation
    rotation
    reflection

 b. B12, C12, B11, B10
    C8, B7, C7
    B4, B3, C3, B2

 c. The shape translated
    3 squares to the right.

 d. It will overlap another
    shape on B7.

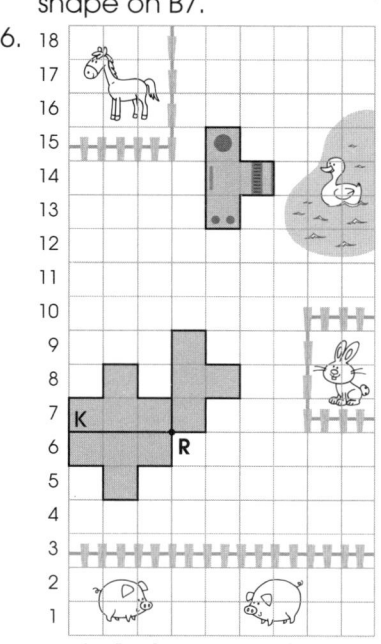

6.

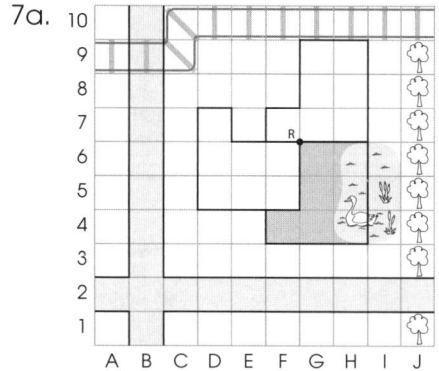

 a. E15, E14, F14, E13
 b. Elise is taking pictures of the rabbit.
 c. Elise is taking pictures of the horse.
 d. A6, B6, C6, B5

7a.

 b. G9, H9, G8, H8, F7, G7, H7
    This suggestion does not work because
    the library is not 1 square away from the
    pond and the railroad.

 c. D7, D6, E6, F6, D5, E5, F5
    This suggestion works because the library
    is at least 1 square away from the pond,
    the railroad, and the streets.

12 Data Management

Math Skills

1. A: 4 ; 2 ; 3   B: 3 ; 4 ; 2
   C: 6 ; 8 ; 4
   B ; A ; C

Problem Solving

 2 ; 8 ; 6 ; 8 ; 6

1. Jake's fish: 12
   Joe's fish: 9
   12 ; 9

2a. Beef ; fish

 b. 1 ◯ = 2 customers
    2 ◯ = 4 customers
    4

 c. 1 ◯ = 2 customers
    2 ◯ = 4 customers
    1 ◖ = 1 customer
    5

 d. Pork: 4   Fish: 3
    Difference: 4 – 3 = 1
    1

 e. Beef: 6   Pork: 4
    Chicken: 5   Fish: 3
    Number of customers: 6 + 4 + 5 + 3 = 18
    18

 f. Total ◯ before order: 9
    4 customers = 2 ◯
    Total ◯ after order: 9 + 2 = 11
    11

3a.

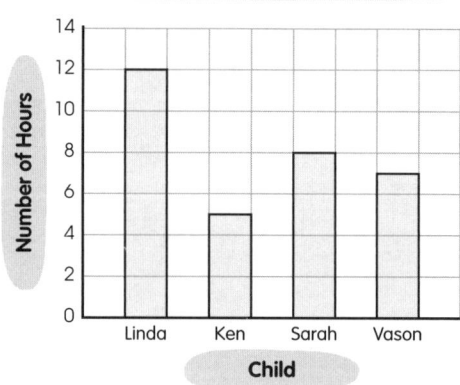

Number of Hours Without Power

 b. Linda's house went the longest time
    without power. Her house went without
    power for 12 hours.

 c. Linda: 12   Ken: 5
    Difference: 12 – 5 = 7
    Linda's house remained 7 hours longer
    without power than Ken's.

ISBN: 978-1-77149-201-0

d. Vason: 7
   1 more hour than Vason: 7 + 1 = 8
   Sarah: 8
   Sarah's house went 1 hour more without
   power than Vason's.
e. Sarah should colour half a block more.

4a. The action genre is the most popular.
    9 students voted for it.
 b. The romance genre is the least popular.
    4 students voted for it.
 c. Horror: 6   Romance: 4
    Difference: 6 – 4 = 2
    2 more students voted for horror than
    romance.
 d. Horror: 6   Action: 9
    Romance: 4   Comedy: 5
    Number of students: 6 + 9 + 4 + 5 = 24
    There are 24 students in Mrs. Lee's class.
 e. Circle graph B shows the same data
    because the action section is the biggest
    on both graphs.
 f. The circle graph should be used because
    it shows $\frac{1}{4}$ of a whole.
 g. The bar graph should be used because it
    shows the exact number of votes .
 h. No, both graphs can show more students
    voted for action equally well.
 i. Mrs. Lee should pick an action movie.

13 Probability

Math Skills

1. impossible   2. certain
3. likely   4. unlikely
5. equally likely   6. unlikely
7. impossible   8. unlikely
9. impossible   10. equally likely
11. likely

Problem Solving

   6 ; 4 ; likely
1a. Total balls: 6
    Even number balls: 2
    unlikely
 b. There are no balls that have a number
    greater than 3.
    impossible
2a. Yes ; are
 b. • a "4":
      Numbers in total: 6
      Number "4": 1
      unlikely

• a number that is greater than "0":
  All numbers are greater than 0.
  certain
• a "3" or a "6":
  Numbers in total: 6
  Number "3" or "6": 2
  unlikely
• a number that is less than "0":
  There are no numbers less than "0".
  impossible
• a "7":
  There is no "7".
  impossible
• a number that is between "2" and "4":
  Numbers in total: 6
  Number between "2" and "4": 1
  unlikely

3a. • a letter:
      Cards in total: 9
      Cards with letters: 3
      unlikely
    • a number:
      Cards in total: 9
      Cards with numbers: 6
      likely
    • an even number:
      Cards in total: 9
      Cards with even numbers: 4
      unlikely
    • a vowel:
      Cards in total: 9
      Cards with vowels: 2
      unlikely
 b. Cards with vowels: 2
    Cards with even numbers: 4
    even number
 c. If the chance of picking an "A" and a "2"
    is equally likely, the number of "A" and "2"
    must be the same.
    2

4a. • a toy dog:

less than half

The chance of getting a toy dog is
unlikely.

• a toy cat:

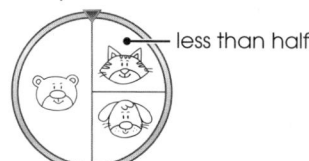

less than half

The chance of getting a toy cat is unlikely.

b. • a toy bear:

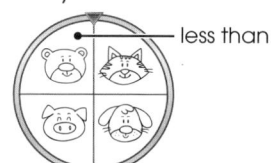

less than half

The chance of getting a toy bear is unlikely.

• a toy snake:

There is no snake.

The chance of getting a toy snake is impossible.

c. • "It is equally likely to get a toy bear or a toy dog.":

the same size

Kayla is describing Spinner B.

• "It is impossible to get a toy pig.":

There is no pig.

Kayla is describing Spinner A.

d. Spinner A   Spinner B

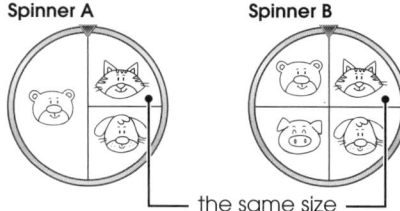

the same size

It does not matter which spinner Kayla spins.

5a. **Jennifer's Box**

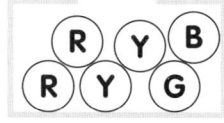

b. Balls in total: 6
   Yellow balls: 2
   It is unlikely.

c. There are no pink balls.
   It is impossible.

d. **Alex's Box**

e. Balls in total: 6
   Red balls: 1
   It is unlikely.

f. Balls in total: 6
   Balls that are not blue: 2
   It is unlikely.

g. The chance of picking a yellow ball from Jennifer's box is greater. Jim should pick from Jennifer's box.

6a.
X	X	X	X	X	X

Chance of picking "X": certain
Jack should mark all 6 cards with "X".

b.
X	X	Y	Y	Z	Z

equal number of → same chance of
each letter   drawing each letter

Jack should mark 2 cards with "X", 2 cards with "Y", and 2 cards with "Z".

c. Jack should not mark any cards with "Y".

d. (Suggested answer)

X	X	X	X	Y	Z

The chance of picking "Y" or "Z" is the same.

Jack should make sure the number of cards with "Y" and "Z" are the same.

e. From the results, half of the cards drawn were "Z". So half of the deck, which is 3 cards, should be "Z".
(Suggested answer)
There could be 3 "Z" cards.

7a. Total trials: 30
   Drawing a candy: 9
   It is unlikely.

b. Total trials: 30
   Spinning a crayon: 26
   It is likely.

c. Picking a car or a candy ball: 15 + 15 = 30
   Drawing a car or a candy card: 11 + 9 = 20
   Spinning a car or a candy: 2 + 2 = 4
   Lucy should play "Pick a Ball!".

ISBN: 978-1-77149-201-0

d. Picking a crayon ball: 0
   Drawing a crayon card: 10
   Spinning a crayon: 26
   Lucy should play "Pick a Ball!".
e. Lucy is correct. After so many trials and having no crayon results, it is likely that there are no balls with crayons.

Critical-thinking Questions

Unit 1

1. 3 ; 3 ; 9 ; 9 ; 8 ; 72 ; 180 ; 72 ; 108 ; 108
2. Square A side length: 16 ÷ 4 = 4
   Square B perimeter: 16 ÷ 2 = 8
   Square B side length: 8 ÷ 4 = 2
   Difference: 4 – 2 = 2
   Square A's side length is 2 cm longer.
3. Highest temperature: 4 × 9 = 36
   Lowest temperature: 0 + 23 = 23
   The highest temperature was 36°C and the lowest temperature was 23°C.
4.

Month	Money Spent	
January	$3.50	⟩ + $0.50
February	$4	
March	$4.50	Eunice spends $0.50 more each month.
April	$5	
May	$5.50	

   Eunice will spend $5.50 in May.
5. 2 small cups of juice: 150 + 150 = 300
   1 medium cup of juice: 300
   1 large cup of juice: 450
   Total: 300 + 300 + 450 = 1050
   Emily has 1050 mL of juice in total.
6.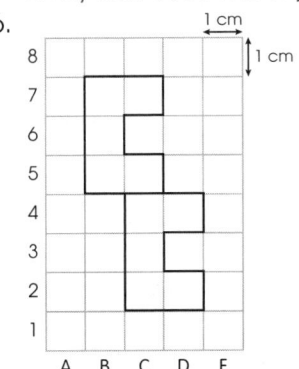
   Squares covered: C4, D4, C3, C2, D2
   Perimeter of figure: 12 cm ⟵ by counting
   The perimeter of the translated figure is 12 cm.

7.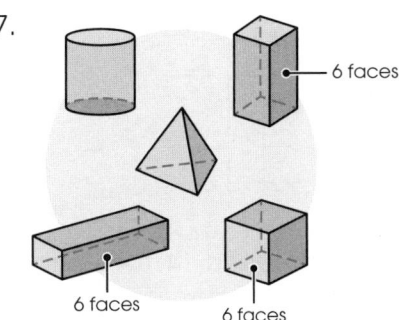
   6 faces
   6 faces
   6 faces

   Nancy's chance of picking a solid with 6 faces is likely.
8. Pairs in 1 package: 16 ÷ 2 = 8
   Pairs in 5 packages: 8 × 5 = 40
   There are 40 pairs of socks.
9. Total mass of books: 2 × 2 = 4
   Total mass of toys: 10 – 4 = 6
   Fraction of mass of toys: $\frac{6}{10}$
   6 kg = 6000 g
   The toys are $\frac{6}{10}$ of the total mass. The toys weigh 6000 g.
10. Students in School A: 200
    Students in School B: 300
    Students in School C: 150
    Total: 200 + 300 + 150 = 650
    There are 650 students in Cityville.
11. "Half an hour" = 30 min

Soccer Drill Days	Total Time Spent (min)
Aug 7 ⟩ + 6	30 ⟩ + 30
Aug 13	60
Aug 19	90
Aug 25	120
Aug 31	150

    150 min = 2 h 30 min
    Chris had soccer drills every 6 days.
    He spent 2 hours and 30 minutes in August.
12. There are 1 quarter, 4 dimes, and 1 nickel.
    Amount: $0.25 + $0.40 + $0.05 = $0.70
    To have $0.50, 20¢ must be used. But no coin has a value of 20¢. So, the chance is impossible.
13. Total: 6 × 4 = 24
    Number of columns: 24 ÷ 8 = 3
    Rick has 3 columns of cars.
14. Stools left to assemble: 40 ÷ 4 = 10
    Stools in total: 234 + 10 = 244
    Mr. Frank will have 244 stools in all.

15.

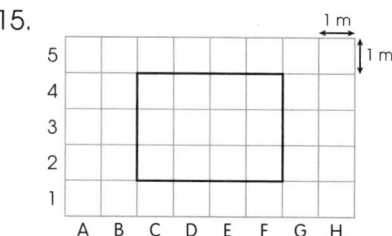

Total fencing needed: 14 m ◄— by counting
Yvonne needs 14 m of fencing.

16. The two attributes both patterns share are size and number of sides. The sizes of the shapes are big and small alternately. The number of sides increase and decrease by 1 alternately.

17. A regular hexagon has 6 equal sides.
Length of 1 side: 42 ÷ 6 = 7
The length of one side is 7 cm.

18.

Total slices eaten: 9 + 8 = 17

Fraction of pizzas eaten: $\frac{17}{10} = 1\frac{7}{10}$

$1\frac{7}{10}$ of the pizzas were eaten.

19.

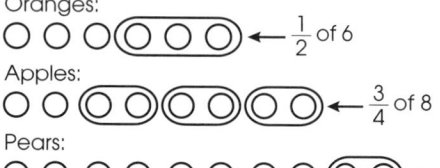

Total fruits bought: 3 + 6 + 2 = 11
Wanda bought 11 fruits in all.

20. Time spent working: 3 hours
Earnings:
$25.50 + $25.50 + $25.50 = $76.50
Mr. Jake earns $76.50.

Unit 2

1. 30 ; 5 ; 6 ; 6 ; 2 ; 12 ; 12 flowers

2.

Day of the Week	Money Saved
Monday	$1.25
Tuesday	$1.50
Wednesday	$1.75
Thursday	$2
Friday	$2.25

+ $0.25   Monica saves $0.25 more each day.

Monica will save $2.25 on Friday.

3.

Time	Temperature (°C)
9:00	3
10:00	5
11:00	7
12:00	9

+ 2

The temperature will be 9°C by noon.

4. 2 big blocks: 3 + 3 = 6
3 small blocks: 2 + 2 + 2 = 6
Bethany should place 3 small blocks.

5. Morning: 15 minutes
Afternoon: 25 minutes
Evening: 20 minutes
Total: 15 + 25 + 20 = 60
60 minutes = 1 hour
Devon spent 1 hour on reading.

6.

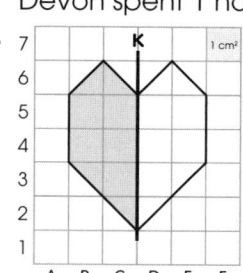

Squares completely covered:
B5, C5, D5, E5, B4, C4, D4, E4, C3, D3
Area: 14 cm² ◄— by counting
The area of the shape is 14 cm².

7. Total milk bought: 2 L × 4 = 8 L = 8000 mL
Thomas has 8000 mL of milk.

8.

Shape	Number of Lines of Symmetry
parallelogram	0
rhombus	2
square	4
kite	1
rectangle	2

Total shapes: 2 + 3 + 2 + 2 + 1 = 10
Total shapes with 2 or more lines of symmetry: 3 + 2 + 1 = 6
$\frac{6}{10}$ of the shapes have 2 or more lines of symmetry.

9.

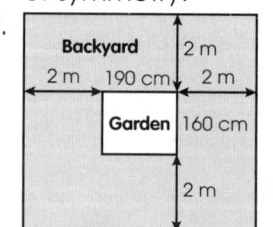

Length of backyard: 190 + 200 + 200 = 590
Width of backyard: 160 + 200 + 200 = 560
Perimeter of backyard:
590 + 590 + 560 + 560 = 2300
The perimeter of Jordan's backyard is 2300 cm.

10. Total savings: $12.45 + $2.55 = $15
Savings each day: $15 ÷ 5 = $3
Heather saved $3 each day.

ISBN: 978-1-77149-201-0

11.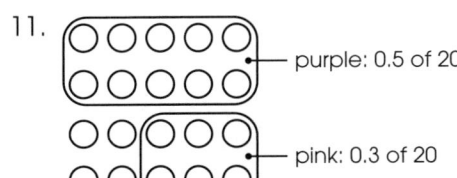
    purple: 0.5 of 20

    pink: 0.3 of 20

    Purple: 10   Pink: 6   Red: 4
    The probability of picking a marble that is not red or purple is unlikely.

12. Total minutes: $45 + 45 + 45 = 135$
    $135 \text{ min} = 2 \text{ h } 15 \text{ min} = 2\frac{15}{60} \text{ h}$
    Caleb spends $2\frac{15}{60}$ hours doing homework in 3 days.

13. Total number of edges: 8
    Length of 1 edge: $56 \div 8 = 7$
    The length of one edge is 7 cm.

14. Total cost without discount: $\$3 \times 9 = \$27$
    Number of discount: $9 \div 3 = 3$
    Total discount:
    $\$1.25 + \$1.25 + \$1.25 = \$3.75$
    Total cost: $\$27 - \$3.75 = \$23.25$
    Jill paid $23.25.

15.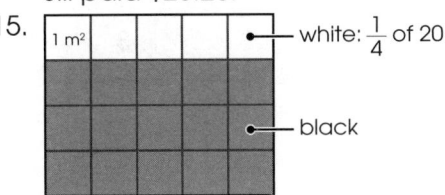
    white: $\frac{1}{4}$ of 20

    black

    Area in white: 5 m^2 Area in black: 15 m^2
    Difference $15 - 5 = 10$
    The area that the black slabs cover is 10 m^2 greater.

16.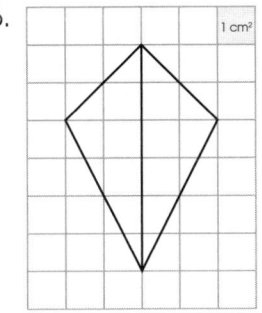
    Area: 6 cm^2 ◄— by counting
    The area of each triangle is 6 cm^2.

17.
Week	Number of Flowers
1	10
2	15
3	20
4	25
5	30
6	35

    $\}$ + 5
    The number of flowers bloomed increases by 5 each week.
    35 flowers will bloom in Week 6.

18.
    toonies: 0.2 of 10
    quarters: 0.7 of 10
    loonie

    2 toonies: $4
    7 quarters: $1.75
    1 loonie: $1
    Total: $\$4 + \$1.75 + \$1 = \$6.75$
    Jack has $6.75.

19. Blue jelly beans: $800 - 127 - 473 = 200$
    200 out of 800 jelly beans are not blue.
    So, it is likely for Hector to pick a jelly bean that is not blue.

20. The pattern rule is: move 1 unit to the right and 2 units up each time.

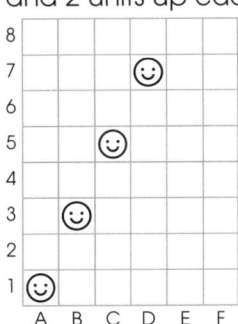

Unit 3

1. 5 ; 6 ; 30 ; 30 ; 3 ; 10 ; 10 trays

2. All faces of a cube are squares.
   Perimeter of 1 face: $6 + 6 + 6 + 6 = 24$
   The perimeter of 1 of its faces is 24 cm.

3. $8000 \text{ g} = 8 \text{ kg}$
   Number of melons: $48 \div 8 = 6$
   Teresa harvested 6 melons.

4. Total number of fish: $9 \times 7 = 63$
   Other pets: $225 - 63 = 162$
   162 pets in the pet store are not fish.

5. There are 5 Thursdays.
   Total spent swimming: $\$8 \times 5 = \$40$
   Total monthly spending:
   $\$40 + \$8.75 + \$6.50 = \$55.25$
   Billy spent $55.25 in all.

6.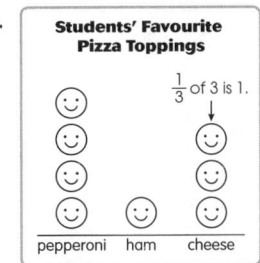

   Students' Favourite Pizza Toppings
   $\frac{1}{3}$ of 3 is 1.
   pepperoni ham cheese

   Pepperoni: 12
   Ham: 3
   Cheese: 9
   Total: $12 + 3 + 9 = 24$
   24 students voted in all.

ISBN: 978-1-77149-201-0

7. "Twice" means "× 2".
Afternoon: 2 × 2 = 4
Evening:

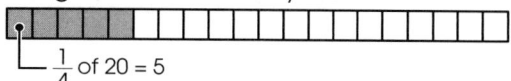

$\frac{1}{4}$ of 4

It was 4°C in the afternoon and 1°C in the evening.

8. Perimeter of frame: 30 + 30 + 10 + 10 = 80
8-cm segments: 80 ÷ 8 = 10
Number of seeds: 2 × 10 = 20
Clement will plant 20 seeds.

9. Length of Ann's backyard:

$\frac{1}{4}$ of 20 = 5

Width of Ann's backyard:

0.5 of 10 = 5

Perimeter: 5 + 5 + 5 + 5 = 20
The perimeter of Ann's backyard is 20 m.

10. A triangular frame has 3 sides. Carlos needs 3 planks.
Total spending:
$12.95 + $12.95 + $12.95 = $38.85
Carlos needs to spend $38.85.

11.

- lime
- lemon: 0.1 of 20
- apple: 0.4 of 20
- orange: 0.3 of 20

4 L = 4000 mL
There is 4000 mL of lime juice.

12.
Day of the Week	Savings
Monday	$3.45
Tuesday	$6.20
Wednesday	$8.95
Thursday	$11.70
Friday	$14.45

+ $2.75
Kyle saves $2.75 each day.

Yes, Kyle will have enough.

13.
Number of Breaks	Time
1	12:45
2	1:20
3	1:55
4	2:30
5	3:05 ← after 3:00

+ 35 min
Stacey takes a break every 35 minutes.

Stacey will take 1 more break by 3:00. She will take it at 2:30.

14.

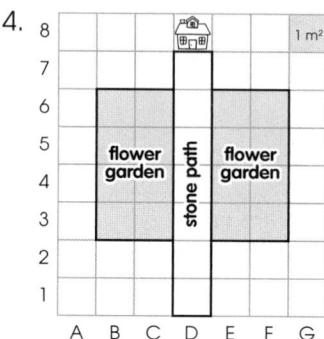

1 m²

flower garden | stone path | flower garden

A B C D E F G

Total area: 16 m² ← by counting
The total area of the flower gardens is 16 m².

15.
Year	Number of Students
2013	100
2014	125
2015	150
2016	175
2017	200
2018	225

+ 25
25 more students attend each year.

There will be 225 students in 2018.

16. A cube has 6 faces.
Area of 1 face: 24 ÷ 6 = 4
Area of 2 faces: 4 + 4 = 8
The total area of 2 faces is 8 cm².

17. Amount 1 person paid: $20 ÷ 4 = $5
Michael's change: $10 – $5 = $5
$5 in fewest coins: ($2) ($2) ($1)
Michael's change was 2 toonies and 1 loonie.

18. (Suggested drawings)

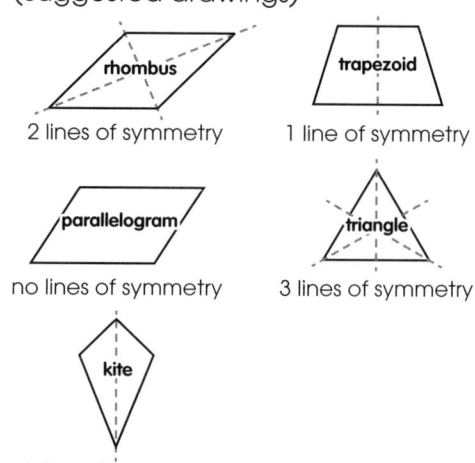

rhombus
2 lines of symmetry

trapezoid
1 line of symmetry

parallelogram
no lines of symmetry

triangle
3 lines of symmetry

kite
1 line of symmetry

The chance is unlikely.

19. Most of the marbles in the bag are red. So, the chance of Rachel picking a marble that is not red is unlikely.

20. Jess: 1 h 30 min = 90 min
Jim: 1 h 30 min = 90 min
Sue: 2 h 30 min = 150 min
Bill: 1 h 30 min = 90 min

ISBN: 978-1-77149-201-0

Boys: 90 + 90 = 180
Girls: 90 + 150 = 240
Difference: 240 − 180 = 60
The girls spent 60 more minutes on exercising than the boys.

Unit 4

1. 60 ; 6 ; 10 ; 4 ; 10 ; 40 ; 40 times
2. Pieces in 1 cake: 36 ÷ 6 = 6

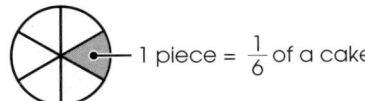 — 1 piece = $\frac{1}{6}$ of a cake

Each friend gets $\frac{1}{6}$ of a cake.

3. Cost of 8 candies: 10¢ × 8 = 80¢ = $0.80
   Change: $2 − $0.80 = $1.20
   Ronnie's change will be $1.20.
4. 2000 g = 2 kg
   Weight of 6 books: 2 × 6 = 12
   A set of 6 books is 12 kg.
5. Small square side length: 12 ÷ 2 = 6
   Perimeter: 6 + 6 + 6 + 6 = 24
   The perimeter of each small piece is 24 cm.
6. Water from ice cubes: 9 × 8 = 72
   Total: 350 + 72 = 422
   There will be 422 mL of water.
7. Cost of 1 basket and 1 bag:
   $3.48 + $2.52 = $6
   Cost of 7 baskets and 7 bags: $6 × 7 = $42
   7 baskets and 7 bags cost $42.
8. Faces on cubes: 6 × 3 = 18
   Faces on triangular pyramids: 4 × 3 = 12
   Total: 18 + 12 = 30
   Jake has to paint 30 faces.
9.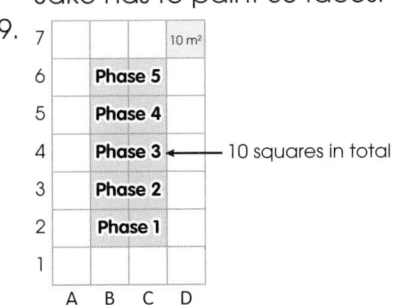

   — 10 squares in total

   Area of park: 10 × 10 = 100
   The area of the park is 100 m².
10. Weight of 1 bag of flour:
    28 kg ÷ 4 = 7 kg = 7000 g
    1 bag of flour weighs 7000 g.

11.
Year	Dimensions (m)
1	2 by 1
2	3 by 2
3	4 by 3
4	5 by 4
5	6 by 5

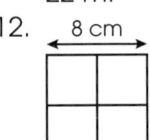

Each dimension increases by 1 m each year.

Perimeter: 6 + 6 + 5 + 5 = 22
The perimeter of the chicken pen will be 22 m.

12. 8 cm

Small square side length: 8 ÷ 2 = 4
Small square perimeter: 4 + 4 + 4 + 4 = 16
The perimeter of a small square is 16 cm.

13. Envelope 1: $20
Envelope 2: $10 $10
Envelope 3: $10 $5 $5
Envelope 4: $5 $5 $5 $5
The chance is unlikely.

14. 20 min:

warming up: $\frac{1}{10}$ of 20   running: $\frac{4}{5}$ of 20   resting

1 hour = 60 minutes
Cathy rested for $\frac{2}{60}$ hour.

15.
	Time	Water Emptied (L)
+45 min	11:35	0
	12:20	2
	1:05	4
	1:50	6
	2:35	8

+ 2

It takes 45 minutes to fill the bucket.

8000 mL = 8 L
Sam had emptied out a total of 8000 mL of water by 2:35.

16. Red: 10   Green: 6
    Blue: 2   Yellow: 4
    Total: 10 + 6 + 2 + 4 = 22
    Green and yellow: 6 + 4 = 10
    There are 6 green and 4 yellow beads.
    Amy's chance of picking a green or yellow bead is unlikely.
17. Tiger: 150 kg ← heavier
    Lion: 125 kg
    Difference: 150 − 125 = 25
    A tiger is 25 kg heavier than a lion.
18.
Time (h)	Number of Pizzas
$\frac{1}{2}$	3
1	6
$1\frac{1}{2}$	9
2	12

+3

Jazz makes 3 pizzas every $\frac{1}{2}$ h.

Jazz can make 12 pizzas in 2 h.

ISBN: 978-1-77149-201-0

19.
A triangular prism has 9 edges.

Length of 1 edge: $63 \div 9 = 7$
Each edge will be 7 cm long.

20. Perimeter of 1 square:
$10 + 10 + 10 + 10 = 40$
Perimeter of 2 squares: $40 + 40 = 80$

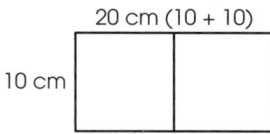
20 cm (10 + 10)
10 cm

Perimeter of rectangle:
$20 + 20 + 10 + 10 = 60$
No, Jane is not correct.

Unit 5

1. 2 ; 5 ; 3 ; 4 ; 5 ; 5 ; 4 ; 4 ; 18 ; 18 cm

2. There are 6 hours between 9:00 and 3:00.
Time in class:
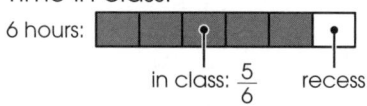
6 hours:
in class: $\frac{5}{6}$ recess
1 hour = 60 minutes
The students get 60 minutes of recess each day.

3. Number of questions: $5 \times 2 = 10$
Time spent on questions: $3 \times 10 = 30$
30 minutes after 12:45 is 1:15.
Perry will finish all of the math questions at 1:15.

4. Cassidy: 2 L = 2000 mL ← more water
Meredith: 1875 mL
Difference: $2000 - 1875 = 125$
Cassidy has more water by 125 mL.

5. Length: $\frac{1}{4}$ of 8
Width: $\frac{1}{2}$ of 6
Perimeter of pool: $2 + 2 + 3 + 3 = 10$
The perimeter of his pool is 10 m.

6. Weeks in 21 days: $21 \div 7 = 3$
1 loonie and 2 quarters: $1.50

Week	Money Saved
1	$1.50
2	$3
3	$4.50

+ $1.50   Jake saves $1.50 each week.

Jake will have $4.50 in 21 days.

7. Juice in 1 bottle: $27 \div 9 = 3$
Juice in 2 bottles: $3 + 3 = 6$
6 L = 6000 mL
There is 6000 mL of juice in 2 bottles.

8. Flowers in small vase: $3 \times 4 = 12$
Flowers in medium vase: $10 \times 1 = 10$
Flowers in large vase: $20 \times 2 = 40$
Total: $12 + 10 + 40 = 62$
There are 62 flowers in all.

9.
Time	Temperature (°C)
11:05	45
11:10	40
11:15	35
11:20	30
11:25	25

+ 5 min   − 5
The temperature drops by 5°C every 5 minutes.
Isaac's drink will be 25°C at 11:25.

10. Students in 1 group: $72 \div 8 = 9$
Students in 3 groups: $9 \times 3 = 27$
27 students went to see giraffes.

11.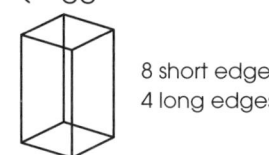
20 L
$\frac{1}{2}$ of 20 is 10.

Time	Capacity (L)
4:45	10
4:50	12
4:55	14
5:00	16
5:05	18
5:10	20

+ 5 min   + 2
The bucket will be full at 5:10.

12. (Suggested answer)
8 short edges
4 long edges

Stick 1 for short edges: $24 \div 8 = 3$
Stick 2 for long edges: $24 \div 4 = 6$
Each short edge is 3 cm and each long edge is 6 cm.

13. Money in fewest coins:

There were no nickels.
The chance that it was a nickel was impossible.

14. "Twice" means "× 2".
Area of 1 rectangular face: $5 \times 2 = 10$
A triangular prism has 3 rectangular faces.
Area of 3 rectangular faces: $10 \times 3 = 30$
The total area is 30 cm².

15.
Day	Total Number of Slices Eaten
1	2
2	3
3	4
4	5
5	6
6	7

+ 1   1 slice was eaten each day.

10 slices:
left: 0.3
0.3 of the loaf was left.

ISBN: 978-1-77149-201-0

16. Total length of 2 other sides: 16 − 4 − 4 = 8
Length of 1 other side: 8 ÷ 2 = 4
Yes, it can be a square because all 4 sides are 4 cm each.

17.

Week	Number of Quarters
1	2
2	4
3	8
4	16

× 2   Pattern Rule:
The number of quarters she earns doubles each week.

4 quarters = $1
16 quarters = $4
Teresa will earn $4 in Week 4.

18. Blue: 6 × 4 = 24
Green: 6
Yellow: 6 × 5 = 30
Total: 24 + 6 + 30 = 60
There are 60 marbles in total. There are only 6 green marbles. So, Olivia's chance of picking a green marble is unlikely.

19.

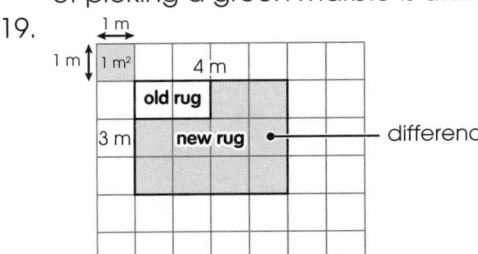

"2 times" means "× 2".
"3 times" means "× 3".
Length of new rug: 2 × 2 = 4
Width of new rug: 1 × 3 = 3
Difference: 10 ← by counting
The area of the new rug is 10 m² greater.

20.

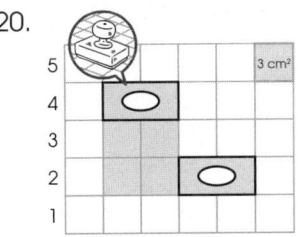

Squares the design covers:
B4, C4, B3, C3, B2, C2, D2, E2
Area:
8 squares are covered.
3 × 8 = 24
The area of the design is 24 cm².

Unit 6

1. Grapes picked today: 10 × 8 = 80
Total: 238 + 80 = 318
Shannon has 318 grapes in all.

2. Books after returning: 2079 + 497 = 2576
Books after lending out: 2576 − 310 = 2266
The library has 2266 books now.

3.

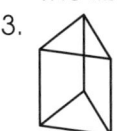

2 triangular faces
3 rectangular faces

Total cost of 3 rectangular faces:
$34.50 − $5.25 − $5.25 = $24
Cost of 1 rectangular face:
$24 ÷ 3 = $8
Each rectangular board cost $8.

4.

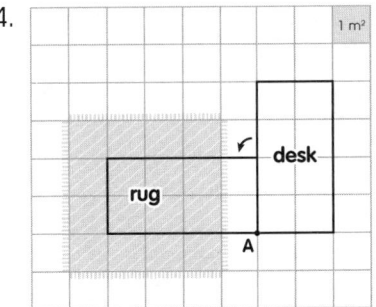

Area of rug below desk:
6 m² ← by counting
6 m² of the rug is now below the desk.

5. Number of books read:
Ada: 40   Bill: 50
Tom: 30   Ivy: 30
Boys: 50 + 30 = 80
Girls: 40 + 30 = 70
Difference: 80 − 70 = 10
The boys have read 10 more books.

6.

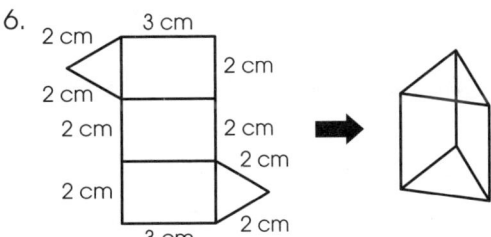

Perimeter:
3 + 2 + 2 + 2 + 2 + 3 + 2 + 2 + 2 + 2 = 22
The perimeter of the net is 22 cm. It forms a triangular prism.

7. 4 toonies = $8
4 quarters = $1
4 dimes = $0.40
Ron's money: $8 + $1 + $0.40 = $9.40
Marvin's money: $9.40 + $9.40 = $18.80
Amount left: $18.80 − $15 = $3.80
Marvin has $3.80 left.

8.

rhombus

A rhombus has 4 equal sides.

$36 \div 4 = 9$

The side length of the frame is 9 cm.

9. Number of stickers given out:

$112 - 94 = 18$

Number of stickers each child received:

$18 \div 2 = 9$

Anna and Tom each got 9 stickers.

10. blue ── green

── red

For "blue" and "green" to be equally likely, the number of blue and green parts must be the same, which is at least 1 part in this case. So the number of parts that are red is 10 at most.

$\frac{10}{12}$ of the spinner is red at most.

11. Total: $130 + 130 + 30 = 290$

1 hour = 60 minutes

290 min = 4 h 50 min

Mr. Smith spent 4 h 50 min on driving.

12.

Time	Temperature (°C)
1:00	24
1:15	23
1:30	22
1:45	21
2:00	20

+ 15 min (1:00 / 1:15) 24 / 23) – 1

The temperature dropped by 1°C every 15 minutes.

The temperature would be 20°C at 2:00.

13. Total number of faces: 6

Number of painted faces: 5

Fraction of painted faces: $\frac{5}{6}$

The chance of getting the unpainted face is unlikely.

14. Perimeter: $24 + 24 + 12 + 12 = 72$

The perimeter is 72 cm. No, Fred is not correct. The shape can also be a parallelogram or a kite.

15.

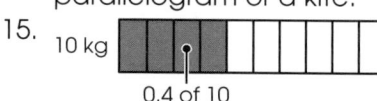

0.4 of 10

Weight of honeydew: 4 kg

Difference: 10 kg – 4 kg = 6 kg = 6000 g

The pumpkin weighs 6000 g more than the honeydew.

16.

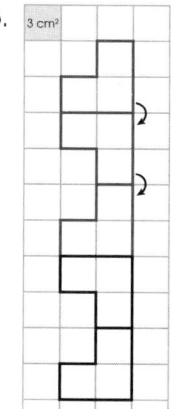

3 cm²

The shape is reflected each time.

Number of squares 1 shape covers: 3

Area of 1 shape: $3 \times 3 = 9$

Area of 5 shapes: $9 \times 5 = 45$

The area of the design would be 45 cm².

17. 2 toonies: $4   3 loonies: $3

5 dimes: $0.50   4 nickels: $0.20

Cooper's money amount:

$4 + $3 + $0.50 + $0.20 = $7.70

Difference: $10 – $7.70 = $2.30

Jane has $2.30 more than Cooper.

18. Half of 4 L: 2 L = 2000 mL

Time (min)	Amount (mL)
30	500
60	1000
90	1500
120	2000

+ 30 (30 / 60) 500 / 1000) + 500

The amount of water increased by 500 mL every 30 minutes.

It took 120 minutes for the bucket to be half full.

19. Number of desks 28 legs build: $28 \div 4 = 7$

Total: $392 + 7 = 399$ ← fewer than 400

No, 28 legs will not be enough.

20.

Day	Number of Toonies Spent
Mon	2
Tue	4
Wed	6
Thu	8
Fri	10

2 / 4) +2   Rachel spent 2 more toonies each day.

10 ← 10 toonies = $20

Amount left: $20.75 – $20 = $0.75

$0.75 was left after Friday.

Unit 7

1. 1 bottle = 500 mL

2 bottles = 1000 mL = 1 L

1 L   1 L   1 L

Total: $1 + 1 + 1 = 3$

Craig drinks 3 L of water.

ISBN: 978-1-77149-201-0

2.

The shapes have a total of 7 sides.

Side length: 63 ÷ 7 = 9
Perimeter of triangle: 9 × 3 = 27
Perimeter of square: 9 × 4 = 36
The perimeter of the triangle is 27 cm and the perimeter of the square is 36 cm.

3. Length: $\frac{1}{3}$ of 12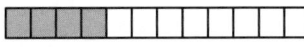

Width: $\frac{1}{2}$ of 6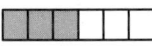

Perimeter: 4 + 3 + 4 + 3 = 14
The perimeter of the new garden will be 14 m.

4.

A triangular pyramid has 6 edges.

Length of 1 stick: 54 ÷ 6 = 9

A triangular prism has 9 edges.

Length of 1 stick: 54 ÷ 9 = 6
Difference: 9 – 6 = 3
Each stick would be 3 cm shorter.

5. 20 houses

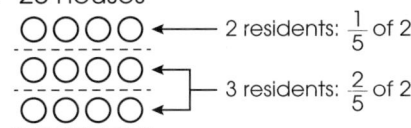

2 residents: $\frac{1}{5}$ of 20
3 residents: $\frac{2}{5}$ of 20
4 residents: $\frac{2}{5}$ of 20

2-resident houses: 2 × 4 = 8
3-resident houses: 3 × 8 = 24
4-resident houses: 4 × 8 = 32
Total: 8 + 24 + 32 = 64
There are 64 residents in all.

6. 1 h 57 min = 60 min + 57 min = 117 min
Number of minutes left:
117 – 37 – 5 – 47 = 28
28 minutes of the movie is left.

7.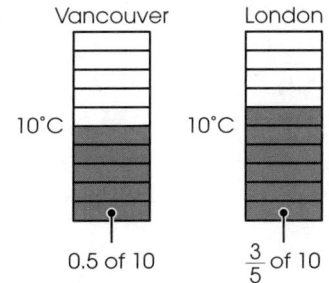

Vancouver   London
10°C   10°C
0.5 of 10 $\frac{3}{5}$ of 10

Difference: 6 – 5 = 1
It was 1°C warmer in London than in Vancouver.

8.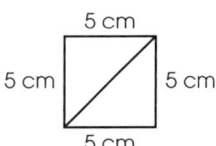

Perimeter: 5 + 5 + 5 + 5 = 20
The perimeter of the square is 20 cm.

9.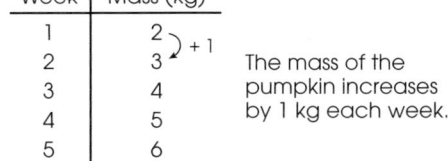

Week	Mass (kg)
1	2
2	3
3	4
4	5
5	6

The mass of the pumpkin increases by 1 kg each week.

Mass of 1 pumpkin: 6 kg
Mass of 6 pumpkins: 6 × 6 = 36
The total mass of 6 pumpkins is 36 kg.

10.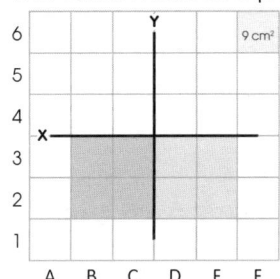

Number of squares covered: 8
Area: 9 × 8 = 72
The area of the painted shape is 72 cm².

11.

September 2016						
Sun	Mon	Tue	Wed	Thu	Fri	Sat
				1	2	3
4	5	6	7	8	9	10
11	12	13	14	15	16	17
18	19	20	21	22	23	24
25	26	27	28	29	30	

◯ = soccer practice

△ = drawing lesson

⬯ = both

Karen had both activites on 8 days.

12. 1 sweater: 500 g
2 sweaters: 500 g + 500 g = 1 kg
20 sweaters: 10 kg ← greater than 8 kg
The rope will break.

13. 24 kg ÷ 6 = 4 kg = 4000 g
1 sack weighs 4000 g.

14. Fewest coins for $5.95:
2 toonies, 1 loonie, 3 quarters, 2 dimes
Total number of coins: 8
Number of coins greater than 50¢: 3
The chance is unlikely.

15. 1023 – 228 + 153 = 948
There are 948 people at the mall now.

ISBN: 978-1-77149-201-0

16. Red: 10
    Blue: 15
    Red and blue: 10 + 15 = 25
    Total: 10 + 25 + 15 + 25 = 75
    10 red cards and 15 blue cards were drawn. The chance of drawing a red or blue card is unlikely.

17.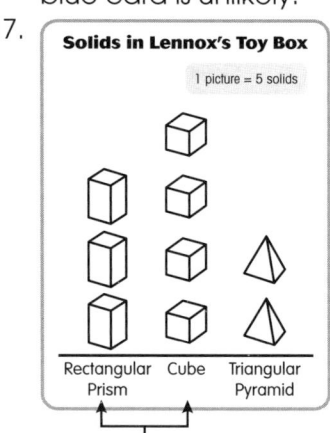

    Solids in Lennox's Toy Box

    1 picture = 5 solids

    Rectangular Prism | Cube | Triangular Pyramid

    more than 4 faces

    Rectangular prisms: 5 × 3 = 15
    Cubes: 5 × 4 = 20
    Total: 15 + 20 = 35
    Rectangular prisms and cubes have more than 4 faces. There are 35 of them.

18. Blue: $\frac{1}{2}$ of 2 ●○
    Green: 0.5 of 10 ●●●●●○○○○○
    Total marbles: 2 + 10 + 6 = 18
    Marbles left in the box: 18 – 1 – 5 = 12
    There are 5 green marbles. The chance is unlikely.

19. Total number of pieces: 8 × 3 = 24
    Number of pieces eaten each day: 3
    Number of pieces eaten after a week:
    3 × 7 = 21
    Number of pieces left: 24 – 21 = 3
    Fraction: $\frac{3}{24}$
    $\frac{3}{24}$ of the pies will be left.

20. Horses needing horseshoes: 120 – 113 = 7
    Horseshoes needed: 4 × 7 = 28
    Mr. Liam needs to replace 28 horseshoes.

Unit 8

1. Zoe's goals: 5
   John's goals: 5 × 2 = 10
   Kelsey's goals: 5 × 4 = 20
   Louis's goals: 5 × 2 = 10
   Total: 5 + 10 + 20 + 10 = 45
   45 goals were scored in all.

2.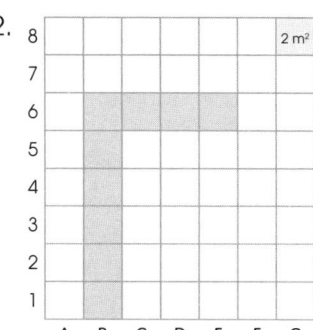

   Number of squares covered: 9
   Area: 2 × 9 = 18
   The area covered is 18 m².

3. 2 L = 2000 mL
   2000 + 450 = 2450
   There was 2450 mL of milk in the carton.

4.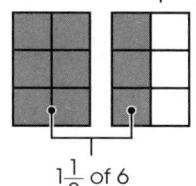

   Number of faces: 8
   Number of unpainted faces: 8 – 3 = 5
   The chance is likely.

5. 2 sheets of paper with 6 math problems:

   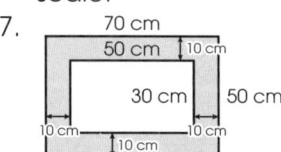

   $1\frac{1}{2}$ of 6

   Number of minutes needed: 5 × 9 = 45
   45 minutes after 12:45 is 1:30.
   Oscar will complete $1\frac{1}{2}$ of the math problems at 1:30.

6. 500 g = 1 block
   1 kg: 2 blocks
   6 kg: 2 × 6 = 12
   12 blocks are needed to balance the scale.

7.
   Frame length: 50 + 10 + 10 = 70
   Frame width: 30 + 10 + 10 = 50
   Perimeter: 70 + 50 + 70 + 50 = 240
   The perimeter of the frame is 240 cm.

8. 3 $10 bills: $30
   Change: $30 – $24.75 = $5.25
   Fewest bills and coins:
   1 $5 bill and 1 quarter
   Lawrence's change will be 1 $5 bill and 1 quarter.

ISBN: 978-1-77149-201-0

9. "Half an hour" = 30 minutes

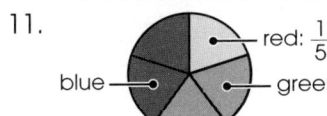

Time (min)	Temperature (°C)
0	50
5	48
10	46
15	44
20	42
25	40
30	38

+5 between times; −2 between temperatures

The drink was 38°C after half an hour.

10. 8 kg = 8000 g
5 kg = 5000 g
Soil left:
8000 − 2500 − 5000 = 500 ◄— less than 675
Mr. Robin does not have enough soil.

11.

blue — ● — red: $\frac{1}{5}$
● — green: $\frac{2}{5}$

The chance is likely.

12. The side length of each triangle measures 3 cm.
Yarn for 1 triangle: 3 × 3 = 9
Yarn for 1 star:
9 × 2 = 18
Yarn for 3 stars:
18 + 18 + 18 = 54 ◄— more than 50
50 cm of yarn will not be enough.

13.
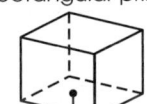
cone   rectangular prism
can slide and be stacked

Only the rectangular prisms can slide and be stacked. So there must be more than 5 rectangular prisms.

14. Total: 8 × 3 = 24
Number of cookies each friend gets:
24 ÷ 6 = 4
Each friend gets 4 cookies.

15. To have the most quarters, Thomas has to have the fewest loonies.
1 loonie = $1
Amount in quarters: $8 − $1 = $7
Number of quarters: 4 × 7 = 28
↑
4 quarters = $1
Thomas could have 28 quarters at most.

16.
Number of Bracelets	Number of Beads
0	754
1	729
2	704
3	679
4	654
5	629

− 25 between beads
3 more bracelets
Each bracelet needed 25 beads.

Leanne had 629 beads left.

17.
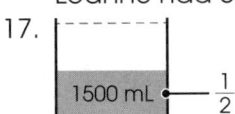
1500 mL — $\frac{1}{2}$

1500 mL + 1500 mL = 3000 mL = 3 L
The capacity of the container is 3 L.

18.
Day	Number of Loonies	Number of Dimes
1	9	9
2	8	8
3	7	7
4	6	6
5	5	5
6	4	4

− 1 between loonies; − 1 between dimes

Each day, he has 1 fewer loonie and 1 fewer dime.

4 loonies: $4
4 dimes: $0.40
Total: $4 + $0.40 = $4.40
Oscar will have $4.40 after Day 6.

19.
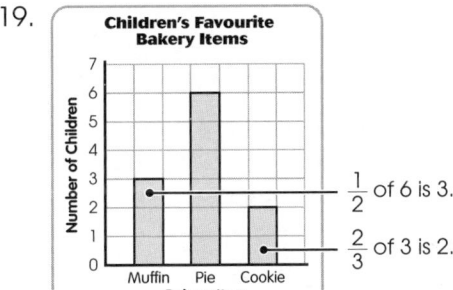

Children's Favourite Bakery Items

$\frac{1}{2}$ of 6 is 3.
$\frac{2}{3}$ of 3 is 2.

3 + 6 + 2 = 11
11 children voted in all.

20.
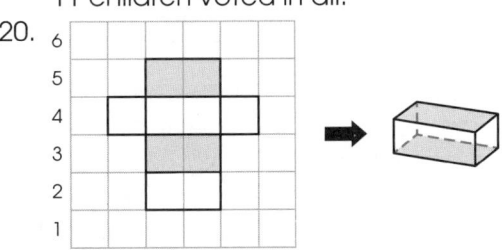

Jackie should colour C3 and D3. The net makes a rectangular prism.

ISBN: 978-1-77149-201-0

Unit 9

1.

apple: 0.1

cranberry: $\frac{3}{10}$

20 juice boxes:

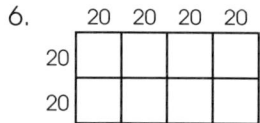

Shelby's chance of picking orange juice is likely.

2. Medicine taken: 10 × 10 = 100
Medicine left: 350 − 100 = 250
250 mL of medicine was left.

3. Cost of toys: $6 × 3 = $18
Total cost: $18 + $4.45 = $22.45
Jason's change: $30 − $22.45 = $7.55
Fewest bills and coins without quarters:

$5 | $2 | 10¢ 10¢ 10¢ 10¢ 10¢ 5¢

Jason's change would be 1 $5 bill, 1 toonie, 5 dimes, and 1 nickel.

4. The bell rings every 15 minutes.
Time:

+15 min +15 min 15 min +15 min +15 min
1:15 → 1:30 → 1:45 → 2:00 → 2:15 → 2:30
                                    ↑
                               past 2:20

The bell will not ring at 2:20.

5. Cost of 5 books: $50 − $8.75 − $6.25 = $35
Cost of 1 book: $35 ÷ 5 = $7
Each book cost $7.

6.

	20	20	20	20
20				
20				

Length: 20 + 20 + 20 + 20 = 80
Width: 20 + 20 = 40
Perimeter: 80 + 80 + 40 + 40 = 240
The perimeter of the rectangle is 240 cm.

7. Weight of 1 piece: 42 kg ÷ 7 = 6 kg = 6000 g
A single piece weighed 6000 g.

8. The greatest difference was between Thursday and Friday.
Difference: 25 − 5 = 20
The difference was 20°C.

9. Total amount of water:
50 + 200 + 350 + 350 = 950
1 L = 1000 mL
No, a bottle with a capacity of 1 L cannot be completely filled.

10.

8 edges

Total edges: 8 × 9 = 72
Mike needs 72 sticks in all.

11.

5 vertices

Total vertices: 5 × 9 = 45
40 marshmallows will not be enough.

12.

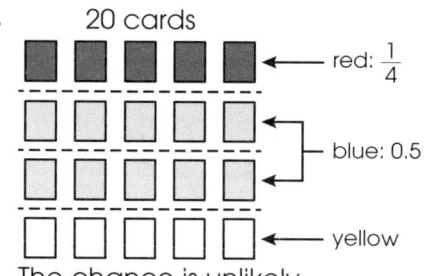

Month	Temperature (°C)
Jan	10
Feb	12
Mar	14
Apr	16
May	18
Jun	20

+2 The temperature increases by 2°C each month.

The temperature will be 20°C in June.

13. Capacity of 1 carton:
500 + 500 + 500 + 500 = 2000
2000 mL = 2 L
Capacity of 5 cartons: 2 × 5 = 10
The total capacity of 5 juice cartons is 10 L.

14. 20 cards

red: $\frac{1}{4}$

blue: 0.5

yellow

The chance is unlikely.

15. Cookies left: 250 − 187 = 63
Cookies for each friend: 63 ÷ 9 = 7
Each friend gets 7 cookies.

16. Audrey could translate it 3 units down or reflect it.
The design covers 10 squares.
Area: 5 × 10 = 50
The area of the design is 50 cm².

17.

	A	B	C	D	E
8				▽	
7				△	
6			△		
5			▽		
4		▽			
3		△			
2	△				
1	▽				

ISBN: 978-1-77149-201-0

Pattern rule:
Reflect it. Then translate it 1 unit to the right and 1 unit up.
The next 3 triangles are located at C6, D7, and D8.

18. Marbles before:

red: $\frac{4}{5}$
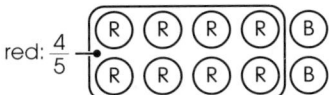

Marbles after:
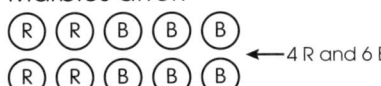 ← 4 R and 6 B
The chance is likely.

19. Possible shapes:
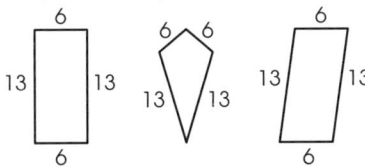
Perimeter: 13 + 13 + 6 + 6 = 38
Greg can make a rectangle, a kite, or a parallelogram. The perimeter is 38 cm.

20. Unfolded rectangular prism:
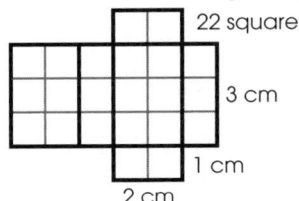
The net covers 22 squares.

Unit 10

1.
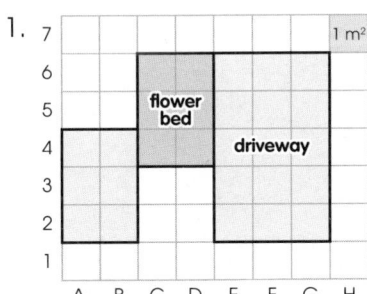
Squares covered: A4, B4, A3, B3, A2, B2
The flower bed covers 6 squares.
Area: 1 × 6 = 6
The area of the flower bed is 6 m².

2. Bowl: 650 mL
Mug: 400 mL
Bottle: 600 mL } 400 + 600 = 1000
Teacup: 250 mL
1000 mL = 1 L
A mug and a bottle can hold exactly 1 L.

3.

9 edges
Length of stick: 7 × 9 = 63
The stick was 63 cm long.

4. Total width: 5 × 9 = 45
Remaining width: 95 – 45 = 50
Number of books: 50 ÷ 5 = 10
10 more books can be put on the shelf.

5.

	Time	People	
+ 10 min (	12:45	0	) + 10
	12:55	10	
	1:05	20	
	1:15	30	

30 people crossed the bridge.

6. blue: $\frac{3}{10}$

purple: 0.1
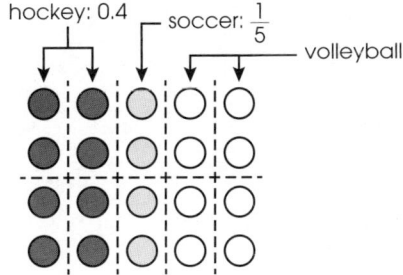

Number of green rectangles: 6
Area of green rectangles: 2 × 6 = 12
12 m² was painted green.

7. Time spent on 1 lap: 15 + 15 + 10 + 10 = 50
Time spent on 2 laps: 50 + 50 = 100
100 min = 1 h 40 min
1 h 40 min after 9:30 is 11:10.
It will be 11:10 after she runs 2 laps.

8.

Time (s)	Capacity (mL)	
1	120	) + 120
2	240	
3	360	Each second, the
4	480	capacity increases
5	600	by 120 mL.
6	720	

The capacity will reach 720 mL after 3 more seconds.

9. 20 students
hockey: 0.4 ── soccer: $\frac{1}{5}$
volleyball

8 students play volleyball.

10. 3 kg = 3000 g
Weight remaining:
3000 – 700 – 250 –130 =1920
2 kg = 2000 g
Laura's bag is lighter than 2 kg now.

11. Total number of eggs: 6 × 3 = 18
No. of plates: 18 ÷ 2 = 9
Riley can make 9 plates of scrambled eggs.

12. 20 beads

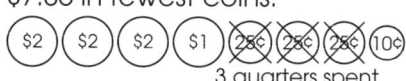

red: $\frac{3}{5}$

Red beads on a bracelet: 12 ÷ 4 = 3
There will be 3 red beads on each bracelet.

13. Weight of crate: 2000 g = 2 kg
Weight of all melons: 18 – 2 = 16
Number of melons: 16 ÷ 2 = 8
There are 8 melons in the crate.

14.
cylinder — can roll
cone — can roll, cannot be stacked
sphere — can roll, cannot be stacked

Solids that can roll: 3 + 2 + 5 = 10
Solids that cannot be stacked: 2 + 5 = 7
Total solids: 3 + 2 + 5 = 10
The chance of picking a solid that can roll is certain.
The chance of picking a solid that cannot be stacked is likely.

15. $7.85 in fewest coins:

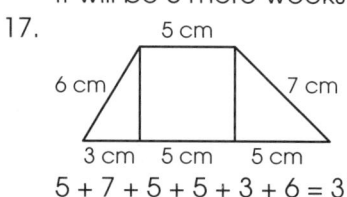

$2 $2 $2 $1 25¢ 25¢ 25¢ 10¢
3 quarters spent

The chance is likely.

16. 1 kg = 1000 g

Week	Mass (g)
1	250
2	350
3	450
4	550
5	650
6	750
7	850
8	950
9	1050

⟩ + 100

6 more weeks

The mass of the fruit increases by 100 g each week.

It will be 6 more weeks.

17.
5 cm
6 cm   7 cm
3 cm   5 cm   5 cm

5 + 7 + 5 + 5 + 3 + 6 = 31
The perimeter of the trapezoid is 31 cm.

18.

Day	Money ($)
1	7.10
2	6.60
3	6.10
4	5.60
5	5.10

⟩ – 0.50

Izzy spends $0.50 each day.

Izzy will have $5.10 on Day 5.

19. Since landing on red or on green is equally likely, they must have the same number of parts.
Possible spinners:

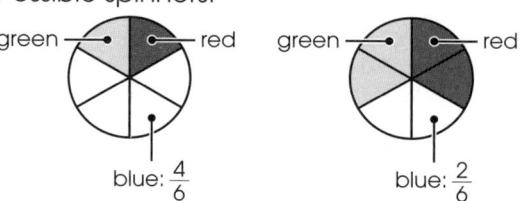

green — red   green — red
blue: $\frac{4}{6}$ blue: $\frac{2}{6}$

$\frac{4}{6}$ or $\frac{2}{6}$ of the spinner could be blue.

20.

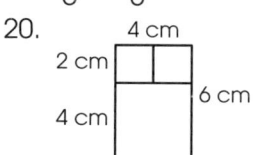

4 cm
2 cm
4 cm
6 cm

Perimeter: 4 + 4 + 4 + 4 = 16
The perimeter of the big square is 16 cm.

ISBN: 978-1-77149-201-0